Creating Us

Creating Us
Community Work with Soul

Peter Westoby

With illustrations by Michael Leunig

Tafina Press

First published in Australia, 2016

Published by
Tafina Press
17 Barr Scott Drive
Lismore Heights, NSW 2480
Australia

ISBN: 978-0-9757658-4-5

Cover design: Tania Lubett

Illustrations © Michael Leunig. Used by permission.
Typeset in Rotis
Printed and bound by Lightning Source

Contents

Acknowledgments

T o the many people who have walked with me on my personal and communal journey; but of special mention, due to direct involvement in this book:

- Ken Morris, for always bringing poetry back into my life, and for being there in tough times, and always;
- Verne Harris, with no words to express the gratitude for journeying together for over 20 years;
- David Denborough, for accompanying me with a weekly phone call during dark days in early 2015; and similarly Lynda Shevellar and Kristen Lyons, for hanging around and being dear friends and respected colleagues;
- Mark Creyton, for the amazing encouragement to be courageous and pursue this topic, for providing public platforms to explore it with others, and for the regular morning coffees;
- Paul Toon, for early reading of key chapters, and journeying on the soul-road, especially for being a mentor and support as I engage in the third quarter of life's journey;

- Pam Burke and Anne-Marie Snider, for giving helpful feed-back on particular chapters;
- Howard Buckley, for 28 years of soul-work together, up mountains, in community initiatives, over rivers, and in co-facilitating workshops on soul and community work practice;
- Allan Kaplan and Sue Davidoff, for being true companions on the soul-journey of 2014-2015;
- Roland Lubett, as a wonderful editor and publisher of this book.

My thanks to you all, and to others who played their part: sorry for not mentioning you by name.

Also a big thanks to Lamington National Park, Noosa National Park, the tea tree healing Taylor Lake at Byron Bay, the Brisbane River, and Mount Barney — all in Australia; and Towerland Wilderness and the Magaliesberg Mountains of South Africa — thanks for being there.

Foreword

MY FIRST ENCOUNTER with Peter Westoby was in December 1992, during a Community Orientation Course with the Waiters' Union in Brisbane. I clearly recall the session he facilitated on inclusiveness and 'open-set' hospitality, with its radical theme of welcoming the stranger. Even then, he was connecting community work with heart and soul. I was struck by his animated energy and by the soulfulness about him.

Twenty-three years later, the composite *community work with soul* has flourished in Peter's writing and practice. He has swum against the tide of shallow technically-oriented approaches to community work, and somehow found the deep amidst present shoals. Consistently, Peter's project has been to deconstruct contemporary community work, and reconstruct new language around how we envision it.

This book is important because its publication occurs at a time when alternate visions of community work are sorely needed. The genius of *Creating Us* is its use of the ancient word 'soul' as a means to animate a re-imagining of community work. With nuance, the book connects the inner and outer dimensions of community work through the language of 'soulfulness', which is an ability to respond from our deepest place. Peter's inclusion of Michael Leunig's visceral pictures further feeds our imagination.

I am delighted that Peter has provided an accessible means for rank-and-file community workers to access his ideas. This book is written for us! I am sure it will lift our spirits at a time when so much of our energy is drained by external compliance and control mechanisms. I am confident it will animate crucial conversations around our community work orientations.

Transformational community work requires an approach much deeper than mere technique. Within my own community of practice, the Melbourne-based not-for-profit Urban Seed, we have begun conversations around soulfulness as a means of re-imagining our practice. While technically proficient, we have needed to slow down and explore the frames of reference informing our community work. Taking our cue from Peter's work, we have prioritised learning and unlearning around orientations such as depth, curiosity, slowness, shadow, hospitality, co-operation, dialogue and solidarity.

Central to this is the process of telling stories around our practice. Stories enliven us by providing means to unravel our work and re-direct our energies. Creating Us discloses some of Peter's story, and profoundly connects head, heart and hand. I encourage community workers to read this book together within their organisations and bring their own stories to it. The ensuing conversations may well transform your practice.

Greg Gow
March 2015

Abbreviations

CBO	Community-based organisation
NGO	Non-government organisation
PNG	Papua New Guinea
TINA	There Is No Alternative
UK	United Kingdom

Let it go. Let it out.
Let it all unravel.
Let it free and it can be
A path on which to travel.

Introduction

A USTRALIAN PEACE SCHOLAR Barry Hill has spent years research-
ing and writing about the life of Bengali poet Rabindranath
Tagore. Hill writes how one morning 'when work was done and
[Tagore had] taken his bath, and as he stood looking out of the window, overlooking a marketplace on a dry river bed, he became conscious of a stirring of soul within him.'[1]

One morning in 2013 I arose at dawn, something I often do, and
felt a 'stirring of soul within me'. That stirring was to do with writing this book. What might a stirring of soul look like, and how is it
manifest? Does it just suddenly and spontaneously arise? I would
suggest that the stirring felt like something arising from the depths.
Ideas and dreams that had been stirring at a subterranean level over a
substantial period of time suddenly assumed some clarity. Something
suddenly becomes more alive — probably it had been 'becoming' for
a while, so to speak. But now it was filled with a new energy. The
emergence of clarity to write represents what François Jullien calls

---

1   Hill, B., *Peacemongers* (Queensland, Australia: The University of Queensland
    Press, 2014), 160.

'a silent transformation',[2] a shift from invisible ideas coalescing at a subterranean level, into a visible structure. It wasn't so much spontaneous, or sudden; but the idea had emerged from a process in which patterns of thought now took on a structural clarity.

That's the case with this book. Maybe 20 years of musing, thinking, writing about other things; and then a 'stirring of the soul', an emergent clarity to write.

An excursion into soul

In early 2009, having written most of a book on community work, my co-author Gerard Dowling and I realised that we needed to settle on a title. We toyed with the language of both soul and dialogue, and played with numerous options. We bounced several ideas off others. We eventually settled on *Dialogical Community Development: with depth, solidarity and hospitality.* However, what has stuck with me since that decision was an underlying anxiety, even a fear about using what was felt to be a taboo word, *soul.* Dialogue seemed more acceptable, and being relatively new writers, we lost our courage and didn't include soul in the title.[3] I have lived with a shadowy haunting since then. In the years since then I have 'girded my loins', so to speak, to write about community work through the lens of this ancient concept of soul. My sense is that the idea of soul offers a perspective that could be rich for re-imagining community work.

In writing about soul and community work I do take the risk, perfectly stated by the character Dave in one of my favourite Australian novels *Tourmaline*,[4] 'If we talk about it, we'll talk crap. This is one of

---

2   Jullien, F., *The Silent Transformations* (London, New York, Calcutta: Seagull Books, 2011).
3   That does not mean I have any regrets about focusing the title of those initial books on dialogue. I am a committed life-long learner about dialogue.
4   Stow, R, *Tourmaline* (Australia: Macdonald and Co., 1963).

the laws of the universe'.[5] As Gabrielle Carey recently considered — reflecting on her mother's life in relation to Randolf Stow, the author of *Tourmaline* — maybe such topics are 'too huge to handle'.[6] I leave it to you to decide.

The purpose of the book

Without good analysis and well-considered strategy, hopes for social justice will be ineffective. Without a strong social movement, social change aiming for social justice will not last the course. Without a new narrative for what change agents dream of, there will be little imaginative traction in achieving social justice. Without new institutions that can carry those new narratives, and provide structure for our social movement, then social change will not be sustained.

This is all true. However, this book adds the idea that without soul there will be little chance of sustained social change. Soul — situated alongside accurate analysis, insightful strategy, invigorated social movements and bold new institutions — is crucial. I write this book conscious of the need for all these 'traditional' elements required for social change, but I focus on the soul element. And I do it with a particular focus on the role of soul within community work, which is one methodology that can contribute to social change.

In one sense I simply write to progressive community workers who want to pause and reflect on their practice, and the assumptions they bring to community work, using an ancient idea that is somewhat hard to define and therefore opens up possibilities and perspectives for conversation.

---

5 Stow, cited in Carey, G. *Moving Among Strangers* (Brisbane, Australia: The University of Queensland Press, 2014), 78.
6 Ibid., 78.

It's a perspective that, in this historical moment, focuses on:

- The *quality* of the work as opposed to quantity (such that when people say, 'how are you going?', we don't have to reply with 'I'm busy', but instead say something like 'I'm not doing much, but I know I'm doing it well and with my full attention');
- The *experience* of the work, and a receptivity to the experience, rather than activities within the work;
- A certain kind of *being* within the work, as opposed to an over-focus on the doing of the work.

This is not to say that quantity, activity and doing are not important elements. However, from a soul perspective, I argue that currently things are out of balance. Soul hearkens to us being present in making community, and in doing collective work with this emphasis on quality, experience, being, and receptivity.

The idea of soul is also imagined as a way of countering the soul-less colonisation of much community work practice by technique, technology and all that comes with it — an emphasis on measuring, proving results, showing impact. Instead, I would like to affirm what many community workers love to do, and how they want to be. But this love and want is often, to the detriment of the quality of the work, squashed by the managers, the technocrats, the bean counters, and ultimately by ourselves in our collusion with their colonisations.

I also try to focus on the role of culture and creativity within community work: the domains of the aesthetic and the poetic. Community work, like much of life, is in danger of being colonised by economics. And economics has already been colonised by econo-*mists*! As a counter to this economic dominance, a soul perspective, at this historical moment, refocuses community workers on culture and the animating elements within culture. These include creativity, spirituality, myth, story, ritual and so much more – as opposed to consumer or corporate culture. In refocusing on culture and creativity, the idea of soul also foregrounds the realms of *imagination*. I want to reanimate imagination in our work. Without tapping into the realm of imagination, then strategy, analysis, institutions, and social movements will not sustain progressive social change work.

Core ideas of soul: metaphoric, mythic, analytic

In a sense, at the heart of my understanding of soul is the idea of animated energies, infused within bodies, minds, culture, communities and actions. Soul is not something defined as separate to mind, body, or spirit – a metaphysical understanding – but is viewed as both a metaphoric and mythical idea, and also as an analytical concept to understand the animating energy within and without.

Soul is metaphoric in the sense that animating energy and vitality arises and can be maintained when people remain agile, responsive to 'shifts within', those 'movements of soul' that I mentioned earlier. Soul requires capacities to attend to those shifts and movements, which in turn requires capabilities in tapping into the depths, a knowing of one's self, or to be more accurate, the constellation of selves that make up who we are.[7]

---

7   Any reference to self throughout the text implies this notion of the 'constellation of selves' underpinned by the philosophy of 'becoming' as opposed to 'being'. The self, framed through a philosophy of being, is often understood as an essence, or a 'true self', as a 'thing' (hence 'being'). Instead self, framed through the philosophy of becoming, is understood dynamically, decentering any notion of true self. The self is *made* constantly and contextually, shaped by stories we have internalised about ourselves, which can also shift and be disrupted, particularly by 'other' stories which represent the constellation of selves 'competing for attention within ourselves'. Bleiker, R. & Martin, L. 'Between consensus and deconstruction: A feminist reading of dialogue' in Brown, J. ed. *Dialogue, Politics and Gender* (Cambridge: Cambridge University Press, 2013), pp120-145.

Soul is also mythic, in that it is a concept that evokes power in our imaginations. Rarely do we hear the word *soul* and imagine a machine, or speed, or achieving deadlines, or achieving more. No, the idea of soul is mythic in that it taps into the imaginative or archetypal energies within us: those that draw on cosmos, spirituality, energy, symbols, the sacred, the poetic, the interior world, and the aesthetic. Soul is also easily understood within stories that are understood as mythic — stories that often 'contain' deep wisdom about the travels and travails of life and love. These include the heroic journey, the rituals and initiations into life-stages, the descent into hell or Hades, the play of the trickster self undoing our well-planned modalities, the struggle between Apollo and Dionysius within, and so on. Myth provides the texture and granularity of a deep cultural understanding of life, not easily captured or understood by simplistic frames of psychology or morality. A soul perspective, familiarised by the language and images of myth, can add depth to our community work.

Soul is finally imagined as an analytical concept, drawing attention to a tradition of critical thinking that sees contemporary culture, economics and politics as 'colonising the soul'[8] or 'governing the soul'.[9] In this sense, soul foregrounds the role of imagination and desire within these domains of culture, economics and politics. It questions what we allow to animate us — what adverts, media, public relations machineries and cultural products.

We have some choices about what animates us; there are forces within, and there are fields of desire created within the social world. There's always the opportunity to work between or betwixt the inner

8   Beradi, Franco, "Bifo", *The Soul at Work: From Alienation to Autonomy* (LA, California: Semiotext (e), 2009).
9   Rose, N, *Governing the Soul: The shaping of the private self* (London & New York: Free Association Books, 1989).

and the outer – negotiating, moving, shifting, resisting, wondering – or we become stuck. Soul doesn't want stuck: it wants to be tested, challenged, fed! Let's feed the soul of community work.

A soul perspective

My musing on what a soul perspective can offer community work has been distilled down to several ideas. Firstly, a soul perspective is concerned with seeing, feeling, intuiting, discerning, deploying and accompanying the energies within community workers, such that the *vitality, quality* and *ethical compass* of the work is maintained. We don't want to go to sleep as practitioners; and we don't want communities to go to sleep. We want to be awake to the world, alive, connected, animated and full of vitality! This wakefulness would in turn require community workers to pay close attention to their own inner lives, aware that the quality of their work could well be linked to the quality of the source (themselves), as well as paying close attention to 'others' (those people involved in community work).

A soulful perspective that is filled or fuelled by vitality and animation at this historical moment might also have a direction. I imagine that direction as downwards, drawn by gravity so to speak, but also with an orientation that is somewhat different to what is imagined as flighty spirited energy. The polarity is one of flight and gravity. Our culture is currently filled with the spirited energy of flight within community work, which can be imagined as upwards towards vision, aspiration, action.[10] Soulful energy within community work practice is posited as different, oriented towards gravity and earth, thereby implying a depth perspective.

10   Hillman talks about spirit in the following way: 'If you look at the language of the spirit, its descriptions, its images- it is always ultimate, absolute, high, the tops of mountains; the soul is in the valley,' in Hillman, J., *Interviews* (Connecticut: Spring Publications, 1983), 16.

Secondly, the perspective highlights ethics, because when vitality, desire, spirituality, and imagination are given legitimacy, there is always danger too. Fundamentalisms and profound intolerances can easily be provoked by such energies, and community work therefore requires a careful, attentive and ethical accompaniment. A community worker won't affirm and accompany all manifestations of soul, not without a critical reflexivity.[11]

Thirdly, a soul perspective is concerned with bringing a renewed emphasis on quality to community work practice. As already mentioned, in some ways a soul perspective represents an antidote to the current emphasis on quantity, speed, technology, technique, outputs, impacts, and results. To be attentive to the animating and connecting energies within community work is to be focused on such things as the quality of care, relationship, effort, thought, analysis, process, difference, and the dynamics of mainstream and margins within a group or community. This emphasis on quality in many ways echoes Otto Scharmer's analysis that the core issues related to social change are actually to do with the 'source', that is, ourselves. And this quality of self is only enhanced through a 'presencing'[12] (a requirement of both presence and sensing) and mindfulness (as opposed to madness).[13]

In writing on soul, I am also aware of crossing into dangerous territory. For centuries, with the rise of the power and efficacy of science, the word *soul* has mostly been officially banished to the realm of faith, new-ageism, mumbo-jumbo,[14] or romantic-poetic literature, although the soul's equivalent has maintained traction within science

11   Gardner, F., *Critical Spirituality: A Holistic Approach to Contemporary Practice* (Surrey, UK: Ashgate, 2011).
12   Scharmer, O. & Kaufer, K., *Leading from the Emergent Future* (California, USA: Berrett-Koehler Publishers, 2013), 29.
13   Ibid., 33.
14   Wheen, F., *How Mumbo-Jumbo Conquered the World* (Harper Perennial, 2004).

under the guise of concepts such as 'psyche'.[15] Danger is paramount, particularly if soul is distinguished from body, spirit or mind – we don't want to return to the old mind-body-soul splits. Danger is also paramount if people understand soul through a psychological frame that colonises soul by a therapeutic culture to be only understood by psychologists.[16] My perspective recognises that while life is psychological, social, economic and political (all traditional realms of community work) it is also in some way about animation, imagination, culture, creativity, vitality, and spirituality; and that life is expressed, or manifest, in our organic bodies, and other organic material, such as the earth. I use soul metaphorically, mythically and analytically, to reflect on elements, dimensions or forms of the animating effect and affect – maybe even the life-force itself.

A final comment: I am offering here some elements of how I have come to understand a soul perspective in relation to community work. I have focused the four chapters on the ideas of soul, soulful, 'soul of the world' and soul-force. However, I do not attempt to build a unified theory of soulful community work. As Hillman asserts, 'soul is ceaselessly talking about itself in ever-recurring motifs in ever-new variations, like music; that this soul is immeasurably deep and can only be illuminated by insights, flashes in a vast cavern of incomprehension...'.[17] As Thomas Moore points out, 'Hillman likes the word for a number of reasons. It eludes reductionist definition; it expresses the mystery of human life ... It suggests depth ...'[18] Central to Hillman's

15   Jullien, F., *Vital Nourishment: Departing from Happiness* (New York: Zone Books, 2007), 58.
16   Furedi, F., *Therapy Culture: Cultivating Vulnerability in an Uncertain Age* (London & New York: Routledge, 2004).
17   Hillman, J., *Re-Visioning Psychology* (New York: First Harper Colophon, 1977), xxii.
18   Moore, T., ed. *A Blue Fire: James Hillman* (Harper Perennial, 1989), 5.

work and ideas is that the soul has integrity – it is 'other', always breaking in, rupturing, and calling. It is energy, a story and a myth, that keeps interrupting. So into this incomprehensible space of imagination, animation, vitality, animation, heart and spirituality, I offer some fresh ideas.

Written to community workers

I am writing to people who might broadly think of themselves as community workers: active citizens, volunteers, or professional paid community workers. You might be involved in your own neighbourhoods – helping out in a school, or with your church, or mosque, or in your community garden. You might be doing some service-oriented community work through the RSL, the Rotary Club, or the local neighbourhood centre. You might be gathering neighbours for annual barbecues, or a group of friends for a monthly reading club. Alternatively you might be involved in more edgy community work, such as Aboriginal solidarity groups, or reconciliation initiatives; maybe you are involved in refugee support or policy advocacy groups.

You might be working within a community-based organisation (CBO), or non-government organisation (NGO), which involves engaging with people, setting up groups, initiating projects or community programs, reporting to managers, negotiating for funding, and related activities. For people doing this as paid work, maybe you have qualifications in community work, or community development – you may have even read the occasional article from the *Community Development Journal*, or attended a workshop or conference.

This book is written for all of you. However, I am assuming that the reader knows something about the basics of community work; otherwise the material might be tough going, and much of its thought may feel a little foreign.

The meaning of community

A key premise for readers, thinking of yourselves as community workers, is that whatever task you might be doing, you are doing it with *others*. What you are doing can be understood as community work because it involves *groups of people* (small or largish) and the work is weaving a web of relationships that ultimately creates what might be thought of as community. Community, then, is not understood as synonymous with neighbourhood, or place. Community is instead something that emerges, as a felt experience, or a social phenomenon, when people *create* it together: when they are in *relationship* within one another, drawn together by a *shared concern* (reading, refugee issues, reconciliation, wanting to garden and so forth). It might occur in neighbourhoods, villages, towns, places; but community is not synonymous with those words.

Poverties and power in community work

I have explained the focus on 'soul'. However, I am also writing in the context of working with people who can be understood as poor or marginalised. Historically, community work has been about a method of social change that is used by the poor to bring change to their lives. They do it through joint action; for example, by pooling small amounts of money to buy in bulk, or to grow their savings, or insure one another against the fragile nature of life; or they co-operate through learning together in non-formal education, or through advocating for a common cause. The point is that they gain power through co-operating. In many ways the community element in community work is about this ability for people to co-operate. There is a huge historical legacy of this kind of work – of small savings and loans groups growing into mutual societies; of reading groups providing the seeds that germinated into community libraries; of small groups meeting to advocate for themselves, morphing into wide-scale social movements.

However in recent years, as community work has become professionalised, the work is not only about a method of social change used by the poor to change their lives; it is also a professional practice concerned with paid professionals accompanying or supporting the poor in processes of change. There is a sense that while the poor have done things really well themselves, they could do with some help. And governments have put aside money to help, so a cohort of professionals is needed to guide how those funds should be spent.

Of course, whenever professionals step in to help, the risk is that the professionals 'take over', or exercise their so-called expertise and end up 'servicing the poor'. In a sense then, without a lot of care, the professionals can undo the need for the poor, or for their energy, to be directed to co-operate together. Then change can easily become a process of the poor co-operating with what the professionals decide to do. The poor become adept in the language of the professionals, their logics, and their industry. The work then becomes very messy. Who is taking action, whose ideas get priority in working out what needs to be done, what vision of life is being argued for? Such questions become central ethical and practical concerns.

The ideas in this book represent an attempt to find a middle ground. It's not about either the poor or the professional *per se*; instead it's about a particular kind of relationship between them. From the perspective of soul, poverty or what is more accurately thought of as poverties,[19] are often manifest in a form of 'stuckness'. There is a lack of animating or connecting energy in the poor to move forward, or if they do attempt to move forward, they find the energy

19   Max-Neef, M., *Human Scale Development: Conceptions, Application and Further Reflections* (London & New York: The Apex Press, 1991).

of someone else, or some organisation, working against them. For example, someone is stuck economically when they cannot get out of debt or find enough capital to start a livelihood. Or they are stuck socially feeling isolated, or cut off; or they have a mental illness and no one wants to be their friend. Maybe they are stuck culturally in that they don't fit in with the mainstream culture and its norms of behaviour, so they feel excluded, hidden, stuck on the margins. Or they are stuck politically, seemingly unable to influence decision-making — it's done behind the closed doors of the powerful, and resources are always allocated elsewhere. The point is that the stuckness means the poor usually remain poor.

Soulful community work offers a perspective on ways forward. A soul perspective explores how a community worker can get close to the experience of a person, or a group, experiencing the kinds of poverties described above. In getting close, they can engage in conversations that might tap into energies and in turn animate movement. A community worker comes alongside into the situation, and drawing on a soul perspective, becomes receptive to what might emerge. They might hear of an idea spoken timidly by someone, and instead of 'letting it go' they affirm that it is a good idea. A conversation is triggered and energy is generated.

But at times the community worker also might need to 'inject' some new energy, particularly if people have been downtrodden many times. For example, most people who get stuck in their poverty have also developed a powerful story of who they are. Prize-winning economist, and author of *Small is Beautiful*,[20] E.F. Schumacher, argues that poverty is to be convinced of your own ignorance. Note that he is not saying to be poor is to be ignorant; in fact the poor

20   Schumacher, E.F., *Small is Beautiful: Economics as if People Mattered* (London: Abacus, 1974).

are usually experts on understanding what produces their own poverty, and their survival strategies often require incredible skills and tenacity. No, Schumacher is saying that poverty is to 'be convinced' of your own ignorance. That is, it is to have acquired a story about yourself. Like any story, however, it is not going to be accurate; it will probably only tell a percentage of the truth. A soul perspective then invites a community worker to create a space in which there might be receptivity to a 'new story', or a way of rescuing a story[21] that someone has forgotten; for example, that they have incredible skills and tenacity to survive. So the community worker, rather than servicing the poor, or 'taking over' – developing an innovative project *for* the poor – instead works *with* the poor, in trying to create receptivity to a new story. A new story is sure to contribute to animating energies, which in turn help people to get unstuck.

Re-storying, which I explore further in Chapter One, is only one way that community work with soul offers to shift the stuckness that tends to make poverties so difficult to overcome. There are other ways, that we will also consider, such as:

- Using arts and cultural work, which unlocks imaginative energy through visual and embodied means;
- Visiting spots of natural beauty such as the bush, beach, or mountains, which unlocks desire and vitality within most people – it's hard to beat a swim in the ocean, or a five-day wilderness hike, to wake us up;
- Developing conviviality and friendship, which gives people a deep sense of solidarity and therefore a platform to hope and try new things;

21 I am indebted to the work of David Denborough at the Dulwich Centre for this idea of 'rescuing stories.'

- Attending to issues of meaning and depth, which helps people to resist the colonising tendencies towards distraction, consumption and busy-ness;
- Developing spirituality, which also provides deep meaning and energy to people's lives, enabling them to both survive a culture often bereft of ritual, ceremony and meaning – making stories (beyond grand final football) and also to thrive in a post-secular society.[22]

I offer a new perspective on community work, one committed to being attentive to both the practice of the community worker and the experience of the poor trying to change their lives.

The story of development — and technology

Thinking about the poor and attempts to bring change, there is a *big* story of the modern era, called development. I have often written about community 'development'. Some of you might be reading this because you are interested in community work, but for the purposes of 'doing development'. Maybe, despite my reflections on the poor, poverties and overcoming stuckness, you see the solution to poverty as development.

From an appreciative and gracious perspective, it would still have been possible to engage with the deeper imaginative energy at work within the notion of development. Development, de-linked from an economic and growth paradigm, could then be opened up to discussions about 'visions of the good life'. However, I have decided against using the language of 'development' as colonised within mainstream development discourse. My motivation has been one of empathy with people who resist or reverse the trajectories of growth, modernity,

22   Tacey, D., *The Darkening Spirit: Jung, Spirituality, Religion* (London & New York: Routledge, 2013).

economic Man, implicated within the model of development – those who opt for autonomy, for their own vision of the good life, even for homelessness, simplicity, the forest rather than the village or the city; those standing against the displacements and dispossessions that development has caused; those who are rendered poor by the measurements and metrics of development professionals. From a 'development' perspective, such people are stuck, needing catalytic change. But I would suggest that they invite, their very presence demands, a re-imagining of ways of being and living. In this sense, I have opted, unlike within my previous work, not to use the term development. Instead I have opted for community work with soul.

Along with development, this book also eschews the powerful mythology of technology within our lives. With God declared dead, and with few places for people to go for a spiritual container, which has historically contained the human impulse for the sacred, reconnection, symbols, myth and story, people turn to other powerful myths for 'salvation'. Development is one, usually heralded by 'progress' and 'economic growth'. Technology is another. From the big-picture perspective, technology is still seen as the future miracle provider that will solve the crises breaking upon us, particularly the ecological one. From a micro-level perspective, technology appears to offer the daily 'rush' of connectivity, assumed knowledge, and freshness. Yet like development, technology seems to be a false god. Despite connectivity and overwhelming access to information, our democracies are losing depth. Decisions are being made with little reference to acquired wisdom, and depression spreads as maps of meaning and deep connections seem to crumble. Not to mention that technology is one of the key causes of the ecological mess.

Soul invites disruption of conventional wisdom. Soul hates rules. The big dogmas disrupted by community work with soul are those offered by development, growth and technology. The big dogmas provide a dominant narrative, but soul disrupts, because it calls people to see the subtle, the latent, even the sacred. Soulful community workers can see afresh through new narratives, which then enables them to be attentive – to see, to hear, to interpret what people say they desire, in whole new ways. It requires attention to energy, to spiritual impulses, to story, to emergent myths.

Community work with soul then asks practitioners to hold the image, the desire, the energy within a group, without responding in the most obvious and routinised way; to let go of those dogmas of development, progress and technology, to disrupt the narratives they provide. For example, consider some of the following scenarios and issues:

- I am in PNG, and some local chiefs want a team of professional development practitioners to engage with the issue of sorcery and to explore its impact on community-level conflict, collaborative endeavours and reconciliation. How do we respond to this? How do we hold the image of the sorcerer, or do we dismiss it with our modern secular impulse?
- I sit with a group of people suffering mental health. They are a part of a mutual help group called Grow.[23] I am there to be supported, and to support them in community formation, a form of solidarity among the imagined weak. But in fact I find myself drawn into their community, made more aware of the fragmented ignored parts of my self, submerged by a busy life.

23 Grow is a community-based organisation that has helped thousands of Australians recover from mental illness through a unique program of mutual support and personal development.

- I reflect on homelessness among Indigenous or Pacific Islander people with whom I have worked. Offering physical 'roofs'
  sometimes helps, but rarely. It seems that the deeper issues of
  homelessness, linked to deeper displacements and alienations,
  are often more powerful than the physical home or lack of
  home. What does it mean, or look like, to work with these
  deeper energies? Do we look closely at the phenomenon? Or
  do we jump to our ideologies of shelter?
- I sit with villagers in Uganda. They have been displaced by
  the activities, the 'green development projects' of a multina-
  tional corporation.[24] Some people see this displacement as a
  wake-up call to try and get a real cash-earning job. But for
  most, it means the loss of livelihood and the basis of life.
  Their loss of land denies access to cultural sites, opportunities to grow food or graze livestock, safety, and security.
  What am I to do? How do I interpret these diverse impulses?
- I sit with chiefs in Vanuatu who are anxious about the
  growing numbers of tourists encroaching on their life, wan-
  dering through their villages, bringing alcohol, drugs, and
  new ways of living. Some of the young people seize upon
  these new opportunities; others are terrified as they see the
  old slipping away. What do I do? How do we view this phenomenon?

I don't offer easy answers to these questions. I simply highlight the
dilemmas of community work that seriously attempts to let go of

---

24   Lyons, K. & Westoby, P., "Carbon Colonialism and the New Land Grab:
     Plantation Forestry in Uganda and its Livelihood Impacts", *Journal of Rural
     Studies*, 36 (2014): 13-21; Westoby, P. & Lyons, K, "'We would rather die in
     jail fighting for land, than die of hunger': A Ugandan case study examining
     the ambiguous deployment of corporate-led corporate-led community
     development in the green economy", *Community Development Journal*
     doi:10.1093/cdj/bsv005 (2015).

dominant narratives and dogmas associated with development, growth and technology. Attending to these questions requires a practice that is in tune with the idea of soul, which I have alluded to as requiring attention to issues such as vitality, quality, energy and ethics.

On the community work role — my fantasy

In essence, then, I am inviting you to re-imagine community work through the lens of soul, one rich with potential.

At this point, it is worth saying that if a soul perspective on community work avoids 'development', then what is the fantasy of a community worker? I suggest that there is a need to re-imagine our fantasy, exposing the archetypal elements of our work.

For example, an important one to expose would be the traditional conception of our role, stated most basely as change agents, and then more carefully as facilitator, or educator, even organiser. While they all contain kernels of the truth, my imagination has been captured by two images that seem to represent a more nuanced understanding of our role. The first is an image proposed in other writings as 'responsive dancer'[25] that depicts the work as one of *co-motion* between community worker and community members. The idea deployed within the image of the responsive dancer is that community workers need to be in tune with, attentive to, and well-practised in being centred in themselves, while accompanying people in the rhythm of change. As stated earlier, I am not proposing strong wilful intervention or 'bringing change', but facilitating receptivity, responsivity and resourcefulness that is linked to the energies of movement, mutuality and mastery.

25   Westoby, P. & Kaplan, A., "Foregrounding Practice — Reaching for a responsive and ecological approach to community development — A conversational inquiry into the dialogical and developmental frameworks of community development", *Community Development Journal.* 49/2 (2014): 214-227; Westoby. P., *Theorising The Practice of Community Development — a South African Perspective* (Surrey, UK. Ashgate, 2014).

The second image is conjured by a Spanish word, discovered through reading one of my favourite authors, John Steinbeck. In his book *Travels with Charlie* (Charlie is Steinbeck's dog) Steinbeck discusses the verb *vacilar*, the present participle being *vacilando*. For Steinbeck 'it does not mean vacillating at all. If one is *vacilando*, he is going somewhere but doesn't greatly care whether or not he gets there, although he has direction.'[26] *Vacilando* is a good way to describe the journey of community work. Community workers have a design and a purpose; we have direction. But we don't really care about getting there. What are crucial are the receptivities, the animations, the loves and the transformations that occur during the journey. I like to think that these musings of Steinbeck could offer new potential for imagining the role of community workers, guiding us into a soul perspective.

Plan of the book

Creating Us is not limited to the idea of community work with 'soul'. Conceptually the book draws on four main ideas: soul, soulful, 'soul of the world' and soul-force. Over the years of thinking about, writing about, and discussing the idea of soul and community work, these concepts became for me the best ways of trying to conceptually separate overlapping ideas. They have provided a structure of thinking that has helped me remember some crucial wisdom. In a sense the four main chapters provide a scaffolding of how the key ideas related to soul and community work can be remembered.

Between these chapters, I have included three interludes. In some ways these are simply indulgences, topics that I love to write about: dialogue, spirituality and resistances. However, they are also included as a way of inviting readers to meditate in a more focused way on

26   Steinbeck, J., *Travels with Charlie* (London: Folio Books, 1962), 53.

three topics that I feel are central to what this book is about. Dialogue implies the need to be attentive and careful in our community work. Spirituality is a way of highlighting the need for community workers to be attuned to subtle and latent energies and imagination alive within people and the planet. Resistances focus the mind on ways in which desire, a concern of soul, is easily colonised by capitalist-oriented consumerist societies. The resistance interlude therefore focuses on the imperative to, and ideas about ways to, resist colonisation, and so re-orient towards weaving the social fabric of community.

At the end I've also included a workshop outline on community work with soul. It might be a useful resource for those who would like to use the material from this book for exploration with others. There is also a YouTube link to a talk I gave at the 2015 Innovate Symposium in Brisbane, which can be used as a discussion-starter.

Finally, ten images from Michael Leunig, the Australian prophet of soul, are included with his permission. For some people, those pictures might be all that they stop to 'read'. If that is the case, then I hope a soulful community work perspective is still imagined with a little more clarity. If, however, the images are read as accompanying the text, then I hope that together the text and images can invoke a new embodied energy to your community work. Enjoy!

Anyone can get a life.
Anyone can lose it
But who will dare to inhabit the thing
And use it?

A lived in life
will soon get loose
and worn
from use and feeling;
Countless tiny scratches.
The shine goes off.
It's very unappealing!

Dirt builds up,
A load of muck and grit
A part of you gets lost —
A hope, a philosophy
Or a love that doesn't fit.

Another broken sleep.
A dream collapses.
A quick repair. It's worth a try.
A scrap of string from the soul.
Perhaps a battered grin
Will fill the hole —
Or just a sigh.

Flakes and cracks!
A major idea buckles badly
A makeshift support is
Invoked quickly.
A tired old joke could
hide the dint.
Or be a wedge, or a patch
or a splint...
Truly sweetly, sadly.

And yet it works and lives!
It all still goes. It forgives.
It's a miracle!
Worn in, bashed in, cried in,
And the great thing —
A lived in life
Can be happily died in.

leunig

Chapter One

A soul perspective on community work

T HE FOLLOWING story provides an opportunity to consider how a soul perspective might enrich everyday community work processes. From the story I then try to distil some elements of a soul perspective, linking to the ideas we've been discussing in the Introduction and that we'll develop further in the rest of this chapter.

In 2012 a colleague and myself were approached by a tenants' union, in Brisbane, to work with them. This involved initiating a community work process with public housing tenants. After numerous conversations, we agreed to use a community-based action learning approach to work with the tenants. The agreement specified that the tenants' union would draw upon its networks amongst public housing tenants and invite them to participate in the project, while my colleague and I would act as facilitators.

Eventually, twelve people decided to get involved, all from local social housing. The project started, aiming for six sessions of community-based conversation and learning, each going for about four hours. The first three sessions were designed by the facilitators, with conversations and activities focused on a vision for community, challenges in community life, and how to get things going in community work. Depending on issues arising, the group could then determine the content of the remaining sessions. The facilitators also explained that the idea was not just to 'learn together', but to develop ideas for group action and turn them into activities or projects. There was palpable excitement, and people agreed to have the first session the following week.

As with any group process, the sessions started tentatively, but people gradually opened up, took some risks, and shared aspects of their lives. In the first week, people used art to draw pictures representing their vision of a 'healthy community'. They also shared personal stories of their memories of positive community. During week two, the group considered the decline of 'community' in modern life, 'joining the dots' so to speak, between personal experiences and larger socio-cultural, economic and political forces. By the third week people were participating enthusiastically, although the facilitators (my colleague and myself) were increasingly aware of their fragilities and strengths – some suffering profound mental illness, others long-term unemployment; others were simply unhappy with their treatment by the public housing department.

In spite of this, the group continued. By the fourth week, ideas for collective action were starting to emerge. The subsequent learning sessions were intended to support the development of those ideas into projects. These included a community garden, a project to lobby the social housing provider to install solar power, and the establishment of a support group for parents of children with learning disabilities.

But as with any real social process, there were difficult moments. For example, during one morning tea break, some people were engaging in 'idle chatter' commenting about people of colour in the neighbourhood. After morning tea the group gathered and one man, from a Pacific Islander heritage, announced that he was offended by the idle gossip he'd overheard, and was considering leaving the group. The facilitators were aware, in the silence that occurred after his announcement, that this was a moment of great significance. Would the group disintegrate into disrespectful accusations, anger and degenerative conflict, or would people hear each other out? It was potentially a moment *inviting* a shift in the dispositions of the majority of participants.

The facilitators, and others, sat on the edge of their seats. I remember my own fear – a voice in my head arguing: *all this good work could be about to fall apart.* There was a moment (a nano-moment even) when I thought: *should I close the moment down, possibly inviting the protagonist to go for a walk outside, or simply suggest a discussion might occur after the workshop?* Yet there was another voice saying, *go for it, take the risk.* As a facilitator, I was looking for the best way to respond, or to create the optimal conditions for a generative response. The moment called for a judgment, and then a surrendering to whatever might unfold from the decision made. There was silence. The man from the Pacific had said his piece; his head was now hanging down, eyes on the floor. All eyes were on me.

Based on a quick intuitive assessment of the group's mood, I decided that it was important to let go of the workshop design and the project goals, and to respond to what had emerged. And that's what happened. The 'event' became central to the possibilities of transformational community work, and a soul perspective ensured a willingness to walk with whatever might unfold from this moment. Good things actually did happen, as several of the 'gossipers' tentatively apologised, and reaffirmed a commitment to social inclusion and non-racist chatter.

There were also moments of hilarious laughter. For example, while we were waiting to start one session, a participant walked in with a ratty old suitcase. We two facilitators looked at each other, thinking simultaneously that maybe a good part of the day was going to be needed to support this person through what appeared to be a homelessness crisis. Instead, at morning tea the participant opened her suitcase which was full of 'onesies'. She wanted people to dress up and have some fun. Some people did, and the next session was held in a state of much comedy.

Between the difficult and comic moments, the process continued – learning, planning, eating of course, and finishing with a celebratory lunch on the last day.

Reflections on the story

It could be a good idea to pause here, and reflect on where you think soul, or a soul perspective, is evident in the story.

Starting at the end, a soul perspective is demonstrated by levels of *fun and humour* within the group. There was a lot of laughter and casual banter, and I find that laughter is a sure measure of soul in a group. Much fun, and a group is probably going well; none and the group is possibly in trouble.

Along with humour, *eating together* is also a sure sign of soul. Sharing food acts as a ritual within the group process, ensuring that both the strategic and task elements of community work are held by the container of relationships. Eating together is a ritual and cultural process with a long history of building community. It's a way of extending hospitality and care, of taking time out of the work, of celebrating a good time.

Within the story above, attention to the sharing of food is central to the community worker's effort. Fun, humour, eating together, and celebrations represent humanising elements within community work. These soul manifestations sit alongside the strategic, or more accurately, enfold the strategic, ensuring that the pragmatic processes of community projects and programs are enfolded in the human process of community-building. The culture of the group, that emerges through particular rituals – in this case, a weekly check-in to see how everyone is going, laughter as someone tells a joke, morning tea, a celebratory lunch – creates a space of soul, in which people start to care and look out for one another. The projects then become secondary, because projects have a beginning and an end. However, the relationships might go on forever, and certainly many of the memories will last. The relationships woven through or within the community work process weave the web of relationships that are core to community life.

Linked to this humanising element of soulful community work, is the *creative* element at work in this group process, triggered through the use of arts and craft. The first session of our community learning initiative involved people working together on collages that could depict their ideas about how a healthy community might look. This creative activity triggers enthusiasm, which is always a good sign of animated energies and resonance. Creative work can be confronting for some people – mainly because people are unfamiliar with it, and it takes them outside their comfort zones. However, it can become a platform for conversations that might never take place if people work only with words and familiar language. The artwork also creates triggers for conversations and story-telling. People use their pictures to tell stories of their vision of the good life, and the picture holds a thousand words. It is quite powerful to see a picture of a community filled with houses, but interspaced by well-worn footpaths depicting a connected locality in which people feel free to visit neighbours.

Also notice the emergence of soul in the first learning session. For example, it is reasonably well known that if a practitioner approaches a community with questions such as, 'What are your needs or problems?', energy will quickly be depleted.[27] The questioning frame will shape the energy available. Soul, as individual and the collective body animated, will sink as people feel overwhelmed by their felt needs and problems. In the story, the first session avoided all questions and concerns to do with problem and need. Instead the session was directed towards eliciting stories of how people would like to be in their communities. Such direction can generate more energy that links people together, and also gives a platform for people to form community and build collaborative capacities, which in many of us are being extinguished within an individualistic society.[28]

The conflict at the heart of the story also represents a manifestation of soul within community work, as it invites soul from several perspectives. From the perspective of the group process, the conflict represents the latent, hidden energies coursing through the group. The official community work process, focusing on the projects and the formal learning objectives that the group and organisations would like to see happen, contrasts with that latent energy that in many ways might represent the real transformational opportunities. For example, in this story the issues of racism and social cohesion could be thought about as significant transformational opportunities. There is a big chance for people to experience difference in a way they have not done before, and embrace difference – perhaps going

27 See the work of the Coady International Institute on assets-based community development for extensive discussions related to issues of needs/problems versus strengths/assets in community work, http://www.coady.stfx.ca/themes/abcd/.

28 Manne, A., *The Life of I: The New Culture of Narcissism* (Melbourne, Australia: University of Melbourne Press, 2014).

beyond a mere tolerance of difference to acceptance, embrace, and actual celebration of the other. It's an opportunity for community to be forged as radical hospitality, as opposed to an emphasis on in-groups, out-groups and boundaries of exclusion. The point is that the conflict represents the soul of the community work process: the stuff of life deeper than a project, the real experience of being with others, the qualitative development of shared lives.

From the perspective of the community worker, soul also repre-sents a willingness to step back from the agenda of the work, and into the experience of what is happening. As I mentioned above, it requires letting go of the urge to control the process, which in this case might have led to a *reflexive*[29] statement such as 'let's deal with this after and outside the meeting'. Instead the community worker is challenged to be receptive and attentive to the emergent energy, is-sues and relationships. Clearly this requires discernment, because the community worker also wants to avoid *degenerative* conflict, which might then have prompted a suggestion to discuss this after the meet-ing. In a sense, the wisdom of practice, which will be discussed in depth within the next chapter, needs to be drawn upon in order to know how to engage with the particular situation as a 'responsive dancer'. As in the idea of *vacilando*, the community worker has a de-sign and a purpose; there is direction, but in a sense the design and the getting there are secondary. What are crucial are the animations, the loves, the experiences, and the transformations that occur during the journey.

---

29   Here I am distinguishing reflective from reflexive. *Reflective* implies a pause, careful consideration, linked to sensing, intuition and thought. *Reflexive* implies a quick reaction, lacking those same qualities of sensing, intuition and thought.

The community worker also has to attend to *being* in the situation
– that sense of his or her own gut response, along with verbal and
non-verbal responses. It becomes central for the community worker
to recognise and accept conflict, to be comfortable in a space of
conflict. It requires a presence to self, others and relationships that is
deeply challenging for many. We will also consider the challenge of
the self within practice in the next chapter.

Of course, conflict is only one source of animating energy that a
community worker has to become skilled at working with. Anthony
Kelly has discussed several others: leadership, pain, gifting and resistance.[30] Along with conflict, these represent five key animating
energies within community work processes.

Finally, and turning to a more mythological way of thinking, I
also like to imagine several archetypal energies at play within community work processes. For example, one would be *warrior energy*
– evident when a group seems to be animated for a long time, with
conversations going well into the night, when people can discard the
despotic local leaders, endure the contempt of the experts, and do
the shitty work often required of community practice with love. Another would be the *mercurial energy* of Hermes at work in a group;
an energy that poet and mythologist Robert Bly argues is crucial for
learning to take place. He argues that 'at some beautiful moment of
the conversation a silence falls that feels mysterious; everyone hes-
itates to break it'.[31] This can be imagined as the mercurial moment
at play, opening up people to a depth of learning that can provide
a sharper analysis of what to do in community. And there would be
lover energy, inviting people to create a warm hearth by the fire-

---

30   I am indebted to Anthony Kelly's work on this – see Kelly, Anthony, *Working
     with Communities,* (Centre for Social Response, n.d.), 139-140.
31   Bly, R., *Iron John* (Dorset: Element Books Limited, 1990), 143.

place and to take care of one another. The *kingly energy* should also arise, giving decisive direction to what has emerged as the mercurial, lover and warrior energies coalesce. Soul in our practice enables us to sense, feel, and experience these archetypal energies at play within the work. Within the story we have recalled, I can remember moments where each of these warrior, mercurial, lover and kingly energies were at play.

Soul as experience and being

Having reflected on the story, let's take a step back and introduce some core ideas about soul from different literatures.

For 20 years I've danced with Thomas Moore's book *Care of the Soul*.[32] It has been a key contributor to my thinking about soul in both life and community work, a trusty companion ever since I first read it when I was 28 years old. It's like an introductory text to anyone wanting to live a soulful life. At the core of the book is the proposal that soul is a quality, a dimension and a movement towards *experiencing* life in a way that adds value, relatedness, heart and substance to life. It's a way of being that requires attention, mindfulness, and presence. It implies going into the depths, the stuff 'under the surface' and into the darker aspects of our lives that at times we prefer to ignore.

Creating Us is a dialogue with the idea of soul in a way that hopes to add the same elements of value, relatedness, heart and substance to community work. In a sense, the shift I am gently pushing for is towards foregrounding *experience* and *being* within community work processes. There is a sense in which many people, much of the time, want to control life. Narrative practitioner and theorist Michael

32 Moore, T., *Care of the Soul: How to Add Depth and Meaning to Your Everyday Life* (London: Judy Piakkus Publishers Ltd, 1992).

White talks about the 'dominant ethic of control of contemporary culture...'.[33] People want to get 'on top' of life, ensuring a sense of safety, security and assurance about what is occurring.

This can also be true within community work. Community workers want to be safe, secure and sure about where they are going within an initiative. Community members are prone to the same tendencies, often attempting to avoid the chaos and complexity of the social world by designing or advocating for simplistic solutions. However, a soul perspective calls us to experience community work processes in a way that often requires 'letting go', being with what unfolds, and radically trusting the process.[34]

As in some of the reflections on the story told above, a soul perspective on community work calls us to relinquish control of the social process. Instead, the community worker is invited to enter the potentially generative 'becoming' space that emerges.

For example, I am sometimes struck with just how lonely people seem to be. Loneliness is a disease of modern alienated society. As a community worker, it is tempting to get involved in a great deal of activity, a way of combating the loneliness. But I wonder if part of the problem is that we jump onto the round of activity too early, too quickly, unable to hold the image of loneliness long enough to consider a 'dialogue with loneliness'. Maybe such a dialogue, informed by a soulful meditation on the deeper experience, would lead to a sharper and more honest consideration of ways forward.

---

33 White, M., "On ethics and the spiritualties of the surface," in ed Hoyt, M. F., *Constructive Therapies,* 2 (1996): 9.

34 I am indebted to a conversation with Sue Davidoff from The Proteus Initiative, who discussed with me the term 'radical trust' which emerged from a lecture she attended of Colin Campbell (currently a practitioner of traditional African medicine, based in Cape Town, South Africa and the UK).

Soul as 'strange other'

Within literature and poetry (the places that are more familiar with the language of soul) soul tends to allude to experiences of life that 'sneak up on us' in everyday life, through an unexpected encounter, a 'falling in love', or a sudden sickness. They are the disruptive experiences, the 'strange other' experiences that many people try to avoid. Mythologist Martin Shaw shares how

> In the space created by strangeness ... is the capacity ... to recognise an encounter with the soul, the silent guest in all descents. This is not soul as a flimsy, intangible idea but as the vehicle ... to bathe in the depth of experience, no matter how hot or deep the water.[35]

In a sense then, this idea of soul invites the idea of 'strange other', that is often not so easy to see or feel or measure. Such disruptive and 'other' experiences occur within community processes that are often uncomfortable, but that represent significant and latent energies coursing through a group or a process. They might be the sudden conflicts that erupt within a community process, or the unexpected analysis that emerges from a group of people and leads to an action that the worker might never have imagined. The disruptive and 'other' might also emerge from community processes that are different, and insist on maintaining their difference, disrupting the 'unity' that a group or community might have been experiencing.

The other might also represent 'another' story to that which a group or community has become attached to, as we discussed briefly in the Introduction. For example, collective narrative practice, as taught by the Adelaide-based Dulwich Centre, highlights that there are at least two stories at work in any group or community that has

35 Shaw, M., *A Branch in the Lightening Tree: Ecstatic Myth and the Grace in Wildness* (Ashland, Oregon: White Cloud Press, 2011), 42.

suffered or been traumatised. There is the first story of suffering: of people's difficulties, hardships and trauma. But there is also the second story of people's resilience, their skills and capacities of survival and thriving despite the hardships. Often, groups and communities get stuck within the first story. A soul perspective within community work practice, attentive to the movements in our practice, understands that it is possible to elicit an 'other' story, or stories, that might need rescuing from deeper hidden levels. The practitioner asks questions that elicit, or reveal the 'other' story, which in turn expands the imaginative literacy of a community. People can disrupt the critical voices – internal and external to the individuals and groups – and become more conscious of their potentiality and other ways of story-ing their lives. These others offer a potentially important counter-story to the mainstream story of a group.

Soul as depth

As well as being disruptive and 'other', soul implies depth – a going down.[36] Closely related to the emergence of alternative stories, soul can represent the latent energies and experiences occurring within a group, a community or a social situation. These energies and experiences are often ignored, or purposefully avoided. They may represent a deeper, more holistic analysis, or a darker shadow perspective. Activist and educator Parker Palmer adds some extra wisdom to an exploration of this mythic idea of soul, describing the conditions that are required to 'see' these depth perspectives. He maintains "the soul speaks its truth only under quiet, inviting, and trustworthy conditions".[37] It is as though people have to slow down to see what might

36   Plotkin, B., *Soulcraft: Crossing into the Mysteries of Nature and Psyche* (California, USA: New World Library, 2003).
37   Palmer, P., *Let Your Life Speak: Listening for the Voice of Vocation* (San Francisco: Jossey-Bass, 2000), 7.

be going on – they have to be much more attentive than usual. As Palmer frames it,

> The soul is like a wild animal – tough, resilient, savvy, self-suf-
> ficient, and yet exceedingly shy. If we want to see a wild animal,
> the last thing we should do is to go crashing through the woods,
> shouting for the creature to come out. But if we are willing to walk
> quietly in the woods and sit silently for an hour or two at the base
> of the tree, the creature we are waiting for may well emerge, and
> out of the corner of an eye we will catch a glimpse of the precious
> wildness we seek.[38]

Palmer's ideas therefore echo Moore's, inviting a careful, quiet and more intimate approach to living and, for the purposes of this book, to community work and interpretation of what is occurring within the social field. To move too fast through life, or through the process-es of community work, is to miss the potential depths, the subterra-nean, the shadow, the 'other'; it is to miss the potential that might be at work within the quiet corners of a social situation or phenomenon. This depth approach requires on the one hand, a need to slow down to 'see' these multiple stories within and without; and on the other hand, speeding up social innovations that shine the light on vulnera-bilities, fissures and soft spots within 'resistance regimes' of powerful interest groups that often want to maintain the *status quo*.[39]

---

38 Ibid., 7-8.
39 Geels, F.W. & Kemp, R., "The multi-level perspective as a new perspective for studying socio-technical transitions", in *Automobility in Transition? A Socio-Technical Analysis of Sustainable Transport*, eds. Geels, F.W. et al. (London, Routledge, 2012).

Soul as humanising relationship

The writings of the Bengali poet and educationist Rabindranath Tagore focus attention on how people relate to one another in a way that could be described as full of soul. Martha Nussbaum's reflection states it perfectly:

> [T]he word 'soul' has religious connotations for many people, and I neither insist on these nor reject them. Each person may hear them or ignore them. What I do insist on, however, is what ... Tagore ... meant by the word: the faculties of thought and imagination that make us human and make our relationships rich human relationships, rather than relationships of mere use and manipulation. When we meet in society, if we have not learned to see both self and other in that way, imagining in one another inner faculties of thought and emotion, democracy is bound to fail, because democracy is built upon respect and concern, and these in turn are built upon the ability to see other people as human beings, not simply as objects.[40]

Barry Hill sings Tagore's praises too, explaining that he was

> the great believer in Welcome. The welcome of strangers, of travellers, of those who were different, was central to his faith, the ethos of his pedagogy, his trust in what it was to be human in peace-sustaining, harmony-making ways.[41]

Tagore's understanding of soul echoes the German philosopher Martin Buber's notion of dialogue. Their work reorients us towards a particular kind of 'community' within community work, one that focuses on the humanising, rather than the instrumental dimensions

40   Nussbaum, M., *Not For Profit: Why Democracy Needs The Humanities* (Princeton and New York: Princeton University Press, 2010), 6.
41   Hill, *Peacemongers*, 180.

of social relations. In our era of hyper-rationality, the soul dimension attempts to foreground this humanising or 'being' requirement.

The humanising dimension also reflects the kind of perspective offered by David Whyte in his book *The Heart Aroused*,[42] where he proposes that the 'soulful qualities of life depend on ... qualities of be-longing'.[43] In a sense, soul as humanising then indicates the qualities or practices that create a sense of belonging crucial to the formation of community, and therefore underpin community work.

Soul as the aesthetic

I talk of soul also as representing the aesthetic-cultural element within community life. Much community work fails to see the elements of social life that connect with art, beauty, symbols, the sacred and belonging, and hence fail to tap into the powerful faculties of desire, spirituality and imagination. These aesthetic elements, in many ways deeply human, are often marginal to the experience of many community workers. A perspective informed by soul, reoriented towards the aesthetic, celebrates these humanising imaginative elements of community life.

Soul as culture

Linked to this idea, David Tacey talks about culture as an expression of a nation's soul.[44] For indigenous Australians, the dreamtime represents the soul of culture – an 'every-time' that is revived and renewed by rituals of practical and spiritual renewal of the land. A cultural lens to community work draws attention both to the cultural-aesthetic dimension and also to the culture of a community group. Almost all community work processes involve a group of people working

42 Whyte, D., *The Heart Aroused* (London, UK: Industrial Society, 2002).
43 Ibid.,15.
44 Tacey, D., *Re-Enchantment: The New Australian Spirituality* (Sydney: HarperCollins, 2000).

together. The culture that emerges from the group is an expression of
its soul – the energies that flow within it, from it, and are allowed to
shape it. The culture is in many ways shaped by the ethos and ethic
that is practised within the group. If the ethos is one of care for one
another, practised for example with regular 'check-ins' at the beginning of meetings, then the culture is a humanising one. If the ethic is
one of hospitality and dialogue, then people tend to be more able to
collaborate with generosity of time and spirit. People give space for
mistakes, and accept things which might be initially felt as annoying.
The culture of a group also tends to shape the spirit of activity and
action of a group – one that is angry, adversarial and ungenerous, or
one that is open, hospitable, dialogical and firm.

In conclusion

In reflecting on soul, in giving such a prominence to its work in community, I am pushing against the grain of our contemporary culture.
This grain is textured towards results, outputs, quantity, measurable
quality, projects, programs, and the 'will' to make things happen:
using technology, coordination, even instrumental creativity. A soul
perspective on community work attempts to invoke a different imaginative literacy. I've told a story, unpacked some thoughts about it,
and linked those thoughts to some ideas discussed earlier. These ideas
are to do with quality, being, experiencing, attentiveness, and seeing
the latent. They require a letting go of control, of the ego-directed
efforts, and instead invite an embracing of community work as a
responsive dance. Community work can best be imagined through
images such as playing jazz, or jujitsu; of learning about being 'in
the groove', or being attentive 'to the gentle nudge of the soul'. It's
more subtle, agile, careful, and unsure; it plays with mythic energies.
It turns the work into a journey.

Soul, dialogue and *Steinbeck's* Grapes of Wrath

I DISCOVERED John Steinbeck's *The Grapes of Wrath* when travelling through a small part of the United States of America many years ago.[45] I picked up a copy at a delightful independent bookshop in Denver, Colorado, meandered into a small café and started reading. I was blown away by the book, the prose, and the imagery used to invoke the profound struggle of an impoverished generation.

I would like to revisit a passage in the book that I have found powerful in thinking about community work generally, and dialogue specifically. In a sense I use it as a Freirian 'code'[46] to invite the reader into imagining and understanding both the dialogic gestures and the formation of community, as crucial moments of encounter between people and initial movements in collective social change work. Also, in approaching this story I am wondering how possible it is as a writer, and for you as readers, to 'stay with the story', to enter Steinbeck's story as fully as possible without thinking in abstract terms. It's a challenge to those used to abstraction, keen to define, rather

45 Steinbeck, J., *The Grapes of Wrath* (USA: The Viking Press, 1939).
46 Freire, P., *Pedagogy of the Oppressed* (New York: Continuum, 1970/2006).

than describe or directly perceive. If you're not sure what I mean by abstracting, hang in there, and read on.

In this interlude then I urge a slow and careful musing over the images drawn upon by Steinbeck. Do you see the people on the move? Can you sense their profound confusion and growing rage as they understand the role of the bank and tractor? Can you picture in your imagination the two men sitting by the ditch, and the gifting from one of the women? Can you perceive the phenomenon of displacement and loss, the experience of poverty? Don't jump to your feelings about it; try to avoid a self-subjective-reflective impulse, and *enter the lives of the two families Steinbeck offers us.* Enter the world of poverty and poverty-making processes that he has presented.

The Western States are nervous under the beginning of change. Texas and Oklahoma, Kansas and Arkansas, New Mexico, Arizona, California. A single family moved from the land. Pa borrowed money from the bank, and now the bank wants the land. The land company — that's the bank when it has land — wants tractors, not families on the land. Is a tractor bad? Is the power that turns the furrows wrong? If this tractor were ours it would be good — not mine, but ours. If our tractors turned the long furrows of the land, it would be good. Not my land, but ours. We could love that tractor then as we have loved this land when it was ours. But the tractor does two things — it turns the land and turns us off the land. There is little difference between this tractor and a tank. The people are driven, intimidated, hurt by both. We must think about this.

One man, one family driven from the land; this rusty car creaking along the highway to the west. I lost my land, a single tractor took my land. I am alone and I am bewildered. And in the night one family camps in a ditch and another family pulls in and the tents come out. The two men squat on their hams and the women and children listen.

Here is the node, you who hate change and fear revolution. Keep these two squatting men apart; make them hate, fear, suspect each other. Here is the anlage of the thing you fear. This is the zygote. For here "I lost my land" is changed; a cell is split and from its splitting grows the thing you hate — "We lost our land."

The danger is here, for two men are not as lonely and perplexed as one. And from this first "we" there grows a still more dangerous thing: "I have a little food" plus "I have none." If from this problem the sum is "We have a little food," the thing is on its way, the movement has direction. Only a little multiplication now, and this land, this tractor are ours.

The two men squatting in a ditch, the little fire, the side-meat stewing in a single pot, the silent, stone-eyed women; behind, the children listening with their souls to words their minds do not understand. The night draws down. The baby has a cold. Here, take this blanket. It's wool. It was my mother's blanket — take it for the baby. This is the thing to bomb. This is the beginning — from 'I' to 'We.'

If you who own the things people must have could understand this, you might preserve yourself. If you could separate causes from results, if you could know that Paine, Marx, Jefferson, Lenin, were results, not causes, you might survive. But that you cannot know. For the quality of owning freezes you forever into 'I', and cuts you off forever from the 'We.'

The Western States are nervous under the beginning of change. Need is the stimulus to concept, concept to action. A half-million people moving over the country; a million more, restive to move; ten million more feeling the first nervousness.

And tractors turning the multiple furrows in the vacant land. [47]

As we resist the temptation to theorise or think in abstract terms, the story provides images that construct the experience of poverty, of families who have been pushed off their land by powerful economic, political and social forces. They feel 'alone and bewildered'. And yet Steinbeck offers a concrete way forward, one infused with potential but inscribed with human fragility. The fragility is inscribed in the story by manifestations of masculinity. Imagine the two men squatting, avoiding looking at one another, trying to maintain some level of distancing male dignity. And yet a fissure cracks the hard fearful masculinity and the two men somehow find one another and turn towards each other. A dialogical gesture starts to form. This is reinforced by a woman's gift of a blanket — an artefact that has 'power' because it's not just a blanket but one that has been passed through generations. This gift comes, at least seemingly, without obligation; energising a hospitality that somehow, somehow, overcomes the inherent hostility that the social situation seems to be filled with. And beautifully the other woman receives it — maybe desperate, or maybe simply gracious and thankful.

Again, our perception of this is crucial, as is our ability to see how we're perceiving. Can we get close to this story, even get within it? What do we learn about ourselves in the activity of interpreting the story? What words or ideas or images attract you, resonate with you? Why might they do that?

Steinbeck gives us a glimpse of one of the crucial movements in community work: from 'I' to 'We', from the alienation of the individual, to community as a vehicle for social change. It's when people find a way of co-operating, or at least initially associating,

47   Steinbeck, J., *The Grapes of Wrath*, 151-152.

that there is the possibility of community formation. But there is not only movement, the formation of community; there is analysis offered too. It's not offered through the dialogue between the men or women, but through the third voice, the author, to us other third parties, the readers. It's an analysis of the original cause of the social situation, that of the tractor and the bank; but also an analysis about a way forward, for people to work together, and grow that co-operative impulse that starts small-scale, but that can grow into a movement.

Now I'd like to invite you to imagine an oral culture with little access to reading. Imagine that those of us interested in soulful community work had no access to textbooks or monographs. Instead, imagine, or maybe try it out – sit around in a circle with a group of friends committed to social change, inspired by what groups can do – and tell this story by Steinbeck. Imagine it as story in the tradition of oral cultures, as a vital tale within which various 'truths' are made manifest through a narrated series of interactions and events. Is it possible to narrate this tale of Steinbeck's to others in such a way that it incorporates itself into people's felt experience; or can the shifts in the characters' actions echo and resonate with people? Can the travails of these two families embed themselves in our own flesh, making the experience of poverty and poverty-making processes more sensuous?

I wonder, if we could hear such story in this oral way, whether it would seep deeper into our embodied selves, etching a deeper experience of the phenomena of poverty, of the fragile movements towards community, and of the tentative gestures of dialogue. This can then be carried into our community work practice, holding us, reminding us, slowing us down, ensuring our practice is more humble, more careful, more intimate.

The story then, like parables in religious texts, can act as a Freirian code – a trigger for conversation amongst groups of community workers, trying to make sense of forces shaping life, not via a textbook, but via critical and careful dialogue. The story invites the reader or listener to identify with particular characters, maybe different characters at different times, and then invite diverse responses. It's not always going to be an easy dialogue. Am I one of those family members squatting by the ditch, or am I an agent of capital – the bank, the tractor, and the owners who are frozen out? But the friction that the story brings to self is hopefully a dialogue that un-freezes us, enabling each of us to be more responsive to the 'other'.

Such memory or story, alive within our bodies, can then sharpen our tacit practice wisdom,[48] adding to our understanding of the structure of dialogue in the story,[49] consolidating knowledge of the subtle but significant shift from I-It to I-Thou,[50] and recognising the latent energies – against community through fear, alienation and patterns of domination; and yet towards community through gifting and hospitality.[51]

48 Dunne, J., "'Professional Wisdom' in 'Practice,'" in *Towards Professional Wisdom: Practical Deliberation in the People Professions.* eds. Bondi, L. et al. (Surrey, UK: Ashgate, 2011).

49 Westoby, P. & Dowling, G., *Theory and Practice of Dialogical Community Development: International Perspectives* (London: Routledge, 2013).

50 Buber, M., *Between Man and Man* (London & New York: Routledge & Kegan Paul, 1947).

51 Derrida, J., *On Cosmopolitanism* (London & New York: Routledge, 2001).

Chapter Two

Soul, community practice and the self

A TTENTION TO practice is crucial within a soul perspective. Without attention to practice, there is little chance of bringing depth
into our community work. Without a reflective understanding of our
practice, we will probably be doing our community work without
being conscious of what we're doing, and possibly be doing a fair
amount of damage. We'll be unconsciously incompetent, the worst of
the worst.[52] There's a good chance we'll be carried along by the tide of
events with little awareness of the experience or how to understand
the experience – of self, of other, of relationships, of context, of the
whole social situation being attended to. We'll be going with the tide,
so to speak, rather than being conscious of the forces at play, the
fields shaping the work, and the fabric of the work (which I discuss
below). Community work practice is one major focus of this chapter.

---

52 Along with unconscious incompetence there is: (i) conscious incompetence (at
least you know you are incompetent); (ii) unconscious competence (basically
good at working intuitively, a 'natural' instinct, tacit knowledge learned on the
job maybe; and (iii) conscious competence.

Also, as I've already said a few times, at the end of the day there is much that is beyond the control of a community worker. They have no control over others, relationships, or any social process that is emerging. They can remain curious to those things, be engaged in them, and respond to them in ways that do have influence. They can influence, but they cannot control. What they can most influence is the self – although from a soul perspective, even that is almost impossible. Hence, the self-in-practice is the other focal point of this chapter. I want to dance between self and community work practice and see what might unfold.

On community work practice

Practice in its most obvious and simple form is what community workers do; but conceptually I like to think of it as 'skilful means'. In an ideal context it is not just what community workers do – with emphasis on their actions – but also how reflective, thoughtful and empathic community workers embody their ideas, that is, how they are, in subtle and skilful ways within the work.

However at a more complex level, practice for community work, like practice in many people-centred 'professions', requires more substantial thinking. To do this I have engaged with the work of Dublin-based philosopher Joseph Dunne, with a particular emphasis on his notion of 'professional wisdom' (and this is still relevant if you're not a professional community worker).

Dunne refers to practice as:

> ... a more or less coherent and complex set of activities that has evolved co-operatively and cumulatively over time, and that exists most significantly in the community of those who are its practitioners – so long as they are committed to sustaining and developing its internal goods and its proper standards of excellence.[53]

53   Dunne, "'Professional Wisdom' in 'Practice,'", 14.

As suggested in this passage, a community worker is not alone, but part of a 'community of practice' that has accumulated ideas over time, and has developed a body of ideas or knowledge that strengthens reflective capabilities. As mentioned in the Introduction, I'm assuming that a community worker wanting to consider a soul perspective already has some sense of the broader knowledge base of the work. They are already connected in some way to other community workers; that is, they're not a 'lone ranger' doing heroic or lonely solo work.

Such a definition of practice also highlights the long tradition of practice in community work that has accumulated knowledge (journals, websites), skills (from workshops, university and vocational courses, on-the-job training), and also various forms of 'communities of practice' such as associations, co-operatives, and networks. The story told in the previous chapter could have ended very differently, badly even, without some awareness and knowledge of this practice. The breakthrough was due not only to a 'gut feeling' by the community worker, but also to some finely-honed learning that enabled substantive reflection. Community workers should make some effort to connect with one another and with these communities of practice, thereby ensuring that their work is not caught up in the latest shallow fashion, but shaped by deeper conversations with colleagues.

However, one of the challenges of these bodies of knowledge and communities of practice, is an over-emphasis on knowledge and skills, with a lack of attention to other elements that make up careful, reflective and effective practice. For example, as would be clear by now, the lack of an imaginative or aesthetic sensibility undermines the community worker's capacity to work from a soul perspective. Captivated by the norms of social and political science, community work can easily become soul-less.

Dunne's focus on practice also brings us to consider what he talks of as the internal goods of a practice. By this he means a couple of things. Firstly, the internal goods refer to "desirable outcomes characteristically aimed at through a practice".[54] What Dunne is saying is that a practice cannot be seen as such, unless there is some agreement about its purpose. Nurses and teachers basically agree on what their practice is — caring for nurses, teaching for teachers. Can we as community workers say what our practice is? It might be described as a relational practice, nurturing social change through connecting with people, and connecting people together. Or stated in terms of purposes, or desirable outcomes, community work practice might include:

- Collective processes of social change;
- Increased confidence and abilities for a group;
- Further achievement of human rights; or,
- A project initiated to the satisfaction of the participants.

From a soul perspective we might add a few more such as:

- Being attentive to and supportive of transformational moments in people's and groups' lives;
- Carefully accompanying groups of people in their search for change;
- Being receptive to the emergent social phenomena;
- Looking for the beauty within community processes.

Secondly, Dunne refers to internal goods as both the competencies and virtues/ethics that "reside within the practitioners themselves".[55] In the case of community work competencies, I could think of things such as 'building purposeful relationships for change', 'nurturing and accompanying a group', 'working with others in the design of a

54   Ibid., 14.
55   Ibid., 14.

project'. In the case of virtues or ethics of a community worker, we could refer to qualities such as patience, humility, tenacity and care. Without these internal goods, a community worker might well end up being a practitioner without a very good practice.

For Dunne, while such internal goods are the *constitutive core* of a practice, there are also external goods, mainly to do with pay, standards, recognition, or what a colleague and I have called the 'architecture of the profession'.[56] It should be noted that in theory, the external goods, or institutional structures of community work, should serve the internal goods of the practice. That is, the professional workshops, journals, and university courses actually help community workers to become good practitioners. However, there is often substantial compromise, as the former tend to colonise the latter. People get focused on the external goods and forget the constitutive core, the meaning of the activities they are carrying out and who they are within the work. Let us all be warned!

It's probably important to say here, that from my perspective I see community work as both an enclave of specialised community work ideas and practice, and a field of non-specialist human endeavour to bring social change through citizen effort. I have elsewhere spoken of community work as both a professional *and* citizen project, to encompass this full and inclusive understanding of practice.[57] So, while talking about professional practice, I am not suggesting that 'ordinary' citizens can't be really good community workers. Quite the opposite: many citizens are very good community workers, and professionals can often be a real problem with their attachments to help-

---

56 Westoby, P. & Shevellar, L., "Beware the Trojan Horse of Professionalization: A Response to de Beer et al.," in *Africanus: The South African Development Association Journal*, 44 /1 (2014), 67-74.

57 Westoby and Dowling, *Theory and Practice of Dialogical Community Development: International Perspectives.*

ing, expertise, doing stuff for people, and so forth. The main point is an assertion that everyone needs to attend to careful, reflective and thoughtful community work practice. Experience alone doesn't necessarily improve practice.

Community practice as immersion in a story

From a soulful perspective, community work can most helpfully be imagined as an unfolding *story*. Imagining community work in this way foregrounds the ideas we discussed in the previous chapter, about experience, being, the other, depth, and the human element.

From this perspective, community work is not necessarily what officially and visibly happens, but is something going on *within* this visible exterior. To think of community work from a soul perspective as an unfolding story, is to think of something that is occurring *within*; it is to bring a depth to the work. In a sense, community work does not necessarily occur simply when the notion of community work is evoked. In other words, community work is not necessarily directly linked to, nor confined nor conjured up by the proposition that 'we are doing community work.' Often, official and visible community work programs or projects do not live up to the claims being made. However, when immersed within such projects or programs, a community worker can discern many transformations at work: remember elements of the story from the previous chapter. Or we may see delightful community work occurring in everyday life, unrelated to any 'official' activities. So transformational work can occur in, beside, or even beneath official and visible community work. A soul perspective brings a curious and careful observation of this. For example, I often find myself observing the apparently casual conversations between people while chopping onions for a community barbecue. It's not so much the 'event' that is the work, but the conversations occurring within the event.

This story-like dimension of re-imagining community work also relates to what can be understood as the 'fabric' of the practice. Such a perspective on practice invites a different way of working to that of 'wilful intervention'. In a sense, the skilled community practitioner is not *imposing* a design on any social situation, so much as *responding* within a fabric of forces, or immersing her or himself in a medium in which she or he seeks to bring about some transformation. In such immersion, the practitioner is always responding to pre-existing energies and movements for (or against) change, and, exposed to the play of chance and vagaries of timing, needs adaptability and a talent for improvisation.[58]

Grounded in soulful community work, this kind of fabric refers to the countless number of ways in which people in a place or neighbourhood might be open, indifferent, or resistant, to what a community worker is trying to animate. The community worker has to confront, or at least engage with, myriad individual and collective tempers and temperaments, along with the complexity of visible and invisible forces at work: material, political, psychological, discursive. What then needs to be considered when thinking about ideal practice is the infinite complexity of the community work situation, of the fluctuating forces at play, and hence the generative or degenerative trajectory that is possible.

In a sense, engaging in a community work process is to enact a story. A community worker, and the people involved, each become characters, responding or reacting to incidents and episodes, together creating a 'narrative thread' that either holds an initiative together,

58 Dunne, "'Professional Wisdom' in 'Practice,'", 21.

or alternatively fails to, with energy and vision dissipating.[59] Hence, every piece of community work practice is contingent on the story, and in a sense can only be understood, like most narratives, retrospectively. The variables that make a 'success story' can never be clearly identified. Eventfulness is inevitable, which in a sense highlights the dialogical nature of all community work practice: the interaction between practitioner and context, with both being (re-)shaped by the practice itself — the responsive dance referred to earlier.

Community work practice as practical wisdom

There is also a dimension of community work practice best understood as 'practical wisdom' that the community worker needs to embrace. In an understanding of community work practice as unfolding story, the community worker cannot fall back on principle, propositions or procedures — they simply won't be enough to either make sense of the story unfolding in a community or social setting, or enable an agile and supportive response. University education in community work does not necessarily make a skilled community worker. They've acquired the principles, propositions, and procedures, but not necessarily the practice. Community work practical wisdom requires the ability to recognise that a situation is either somewhat typical, that is, a situation that has been met before and for which there is some kind of method, or already established 'way forward'; or that the situation is not typical, *but* that the practitioner is capable of responding adequately and appropriately — and things might still not work out well.

In doing this there is recognition that every situation needs to be respected in its particularity, but at the same time, recognition that the practitioner (with wisdom) is able to 'bring this particularity into

59 Westoby and Kaplan, "Foregrounding Practice" 10.

some relationship, albeit one yet to be determined, with the body of [community work] knowledge ... one's adeptness then lies then in the capacity to mediate between the general and the particular'.[60] This in turn requires the capacity to engage each and every situation with fresh creative insight, knowing that the particular context should always shape any kind of response. It also entails the recognition that such a way of responding requires a radical openness that 'allows one's experience to be quickened by new learning so that one develops finely discriminating judgement'.[61] In doing this there is a receptivity to the salient moment, knowing that receptivity might 'call for a high level of imagination and emotional engagement by the self',[62] which in turn acknowledges that judgement in the moment is a confluence of both the personal and professional, expressive of the kind of person as well as the kind of practitioner that one has become.

Finally, from a soul perspective, there is awareness that community work practice is often more about 'artistry'[63] than about design; and that this artistry is recognised as an embodied responsiveness.[64] Therefore practice becomes the ability to skilfully dance the dance of relationship, being present and responsive to other, context and history, yet also being intuitive, empathic, careful, thoughtful, creative, playful and disciplined.

The self in community practice

For a community worker to be consciously drawing on professional wisdom within the unfolding story or fabric of any community work

---

60   Dunne, "'Professional Wisdom' in 'Practice,'" 18.
61   Ibid., 18.
62   Ibid., 19.
63   Schon, D., *The Reflective Practitioner: How Professionals Think in Action* (London: Ashgate, 1983); Kaplan, A., *Development Practitioners and Social Process: Artists of the Invisible* (Chicago & London: Pluto Press, 2002).
64   Westoby & Kaplan, "Foregrounding Practice," 221.

project or process, they need to cultivate a strong awareness of self. A soul perspective on community practice invites a commitment to be attentive to the self, the source, and what Hillman calls interiority. Without this cultivation and commitment, a community worker can become a 'problem' within the story, either disrupting the potential at work, or simply being ineffective.

The self, whilst a slippery notion, at least invites the necessity to be conscious of habits, practices and disciplines such as:

- Emotional responses: noticing when we're feeling fear, anxiety or anger in a social situation or community work process, and noticing where these feelings arise, often as sensations within the body;[65] and then carefully pausing and checking how those feelings are being manifest in the work – as destructive, distracting, or as helpful guides);
- The tendency to drift away from the situation at hand, to no longer be present to what is going on, to be wishing the meeting was over, or that someone who is annoying would 'shut up' (when that person represents a component of the social situation, maybe even that important 'other' perspective);
- Leaps to interpret what we see, usually what the 'ego' sees as a superficial assessment of what is going on within a social situation or community work process, and therefore not an accurate interpretation;

---

65 I recently sat in a delightful workshop led by Carol Perry, who taught us how our body gives us access to our imagined centre, and it's often in this centre, along with our emotional awareness and reflection, that we can access our intuitive wisdom.

- An orientation to control, to want something to move along as planned, or to impose an analysis that is already pre-determined or assumed.

Overall, the invitation is to cultivate an interior life, such that we are practised in being aware of these feelings, sensations, leaps and tendencies. Without a practised interior life, community workers tend to 'go with the flow', unconsciously reacting, interpreting and drifting.

This last point highlights David Tacey's argument that 'undervaluation of soul is a fear of interiority'.[66] Within a globalising culture that is overly secular – often devoid of soul – interiority is routinely avoided. This tendency can be amplified within the world of community workers, especially those with an activist tendency.

A soul perspective invites such community workers to bring interiority into their work, a reflective space to look at themselves as well as the other. A soul-oriented community worker who is cultivating an awareness of self and interiority, also cultivates an awareness of the other, along with his or her own response to the other within the social situation. In the previous chapter, we discussed the kinds of 'other' in community work – people who are different, or who offer a different analysis. What becomes crucial is to be conscious of responses or reactions to the other. Any arising feeling is legitimate; however, the danger lies in acting in an unconscious way on those feelings. All the things that we ourselves are trying to recognise in ourselves – our feelings, our leaps to interpretation, our tendencies to drift away – are also manifest in others. A community worker needs to be conscious of his or her own response to those manifestations. No community worker will be fully conscious of self, or of the other, but attempts will surely make the work more fruitful.

66   Tacey, *The Darkening Spirit: Jung, Spirituality, Religion*, 66.

Being aware of self is also enfolded within attentiveness to the relationships between self and other people. Is there trust, or a growing trust, or is there suspicion? Is there a grace and generosity between people when they let one another down? Do people support one another's ideas, or knock them down? Is the culture of the emergent group supportive of task, strategy and relationship? Are we as practitioners attentive and aware of our own personal investment in any community work outcomes, and therefore do we ensure that we are not dominating or manipulating? There is a sense in which we have to hold the tension between being passionate 'responsive dancers' and yet being detached from outcomes, so that we can walk at the pace and in the direction of the people, not our own.

Finally, within this awareness of self, other, relations, is the need to be conscious of our own practice. How are we in the work? What happens when the unexpected occurs? What do we do when challenged by community members (our role, our analysis, our ideas of a way forward)? What fantasy are we enacting in a particular story of community work? Are we drawing on the wisdom and experience learned over many years? In what way do we think about our use of power in community work?

Skilled and soulful power

With this last question in mind, I want to shine a little light on this key issue of power within our practice. As mentioned in the Introduction, community work is a methodology of the poor to overcome powerlessness. Their power is generally gained through working in groups, in collaborative forms of power. Power is central to our work. However, in this section I want to focus not on people's power, but on the *community worker's power*. In many ways the interface between the self, practice and awareness requires a careful understanding of our own power as community workers. The attitudes and behaviour of a community worker within the community work fabric will greatly influence or shape the story that occurs.

Thomas Moore and Jack Kornfield provide some useful ways of thinking about this through naming two types of power through the lens of soul. For Moore, heroic-egotistical power is contrasted with soulful power,[67] while Kornfield contrasts unskilled-painful power with skilled power.[68] The qualities of heroic-egotistical and unskilled-painful types of power tend to be grasping, greed, longing and inadequacy; while the qualities of soulful-skilled types of power are those of creativity, wisdom, vitality, love and compassion – all part of my conception of soul.

It is important to recognise that conceptualising power in these dualistic ways is not about a moral choice of one over the other. The actual substantive forms of power within our practice will be more or less the same, but there will be a subtle shift in the nature of the power exercised, the energy behind the power. Community workers have options within their exercise of power; the need is to bring an acute attention to this process. The exercise of skilled and soulful power calls for moral examination: not a moralistic desire for pure motives, but a desire for awareness and depth, enabling clarity and transforming choice. Such an examination enables a shift in the energy behind community work – bringing depth to the practice.

---

67   Moore, T., *Care of the Soul: How to Add Depth and Meaning to Your Everyday Life*.
68   Kornfield, J., *A Path With Heart* (USA & Canada: Bantam Books, 1993).

Dangers of unskilled and soul-less power

In bringing this kind of attentiveness to the exercise of power, it can be helpful to name some of the dangers that lie within unskilled and heroic power that can easily trip community workers up, and contrast them with the attributes of soulful-skilful power.

The first danger is *narcissism*. This danger refers to the heroic self-interest that can captivate a community worker where the practice is not grounded in love and lacks a moral commitment. There is a danger that community workers become attached to the image or collective persona of being activists, rather than being motivated by care for people's well-being and responsive to them. The collective ideology becomes primary, and the being or making of community secondary. In contrast, soulful-skilful power avoids becoming captive to the ego or image of being a community activist. The community worker might be aware of that part of the self that is seeking some ego recognition, or enjoying the image. In that awareness, they tender carefully the human need for belonging and love, but they keep the focus of the work on the real purpose.

The second danger is *we become what we hate*. Within the exercising of power there lies a powerful shadow. While usually committed to dialogical or co-operative processes, community work may also engage in conflict. This can be with members of a group that a community worker is accompanying, or those who are quite literally opponents – for example in a community campaign. In using energy against people seen as adversaries, opponents or enemies, there is a risk of becoming in many ways the same as them. This is true of psychological dynamics. For example, an alcoholic who fights against being an alcoholic can actually give energy to the addiction. The 'hating of the alcoholic within' leads down the road of alcoholism. Walter Wink, in his ground-breaking theological treatise *Engaging the*

Powers,[69] demonstrates how this process is equally true in the social world. Wink discusses in depth an example of how the Allies, during World War II, became as 'hateful' as the German army, climaxing in the abominable bombing of Dresden. The warning here is to be very careful in our practice of power. What are the motivations and energies feeding our work, our participation, and our confrontations with the 'other' powers?

The third danger is *passivity*. Egotistically-oriented acts of power may reflect a deep inner passivity. The outer energy can have a shadow of inner emptiness. Soul-inspired action is action filled with passion and vitality. In contrast, an action that is simply an attempt to flee our own passivity and emptiness is unskilled. People simply 'jump on a bandwagon', and their involvement in action brings the danger of shallowness, of lack of reflection, of bypassing deep values and commitments.

Naming these dangers enables community workers to take precautions. We can question the energy behind our use of power in a particular situation. Are our desires, which legitimise our exercise of power, simply rationalisations for narcissism? Are they simply heroic attempts to escape our passivity rather than soulful, passionate attempts to build community? Is the power exercised transforming us into the images and practices of our enemies?

Reflective, soul-oriented practice requires an understanding of our own innocence, denial, and belief. We may believe we are too innocent to become like the enemy. We deny our own shadows and hold to the belief that our crusade or exercise of power is grounded in truth. We need to stop and reflect with an honesty that acknowledges

69   Wink, W., *Engaging the Powers: Discernment and Resistance in a World of Domination* (Minneapolis: Fortress Press, 1992).

not only the energy of compassion, anger and wisdom, but also the possible energies of narcissism, violence and longing. We might not be so different from the enemy – in their position we could well do the same. But our entry into an awareness that enables us to debunk our own innocence, and be free from our denials, will enable us to transform the kind of power we exercise.

A story

The following story may illustrate these issues. During the writing of some of this book, I have been involved in a significant local campaign. One element of the campaign has consisted of building an alliance of residents, community organisations and political groups advocating against the proposed 'development plan' of several levels of government. At the same time the alliance is advocating for an alternative plan, more people-oriented, with a different vision of open space, building size, public transport, and availability of services. I have been in the thick of the debate, occasionally chairing what has evolved as regular reflection/planning meetings of the alliance. The task has been a test of my practice, and has also required an astute sense of self within the work along with a commitment to interiority, ensuring I don't react too impulsively to unfolding events.

We can draw on two incidents during the sixth week of the campaign to examine issues of practice and self. Firstly, during the planning meeting there was a discussion about the use of a growing number of 'expert' briefs. As background, the alliance had convened an experts' group in the third week of the campaign, and numerous experts were preparing two-page briefs of their expertise (open space design, urban planning, engineering, cultural planning and so forth). One person on the expert group, also the chair of a 'powerful' local community organisation, had set up a 'cloud storage' shared folder for those expert papers. When people in the alliance asked to access those papers, that is, could they be invited to join the shared folder, the person said "no, the experts don't want their work shared so that it can be used by anyone." I knew that this was not true in all cases. Some did want careful restrictions on access to their work; others weren't bothered, wanting their work to be shared as widely as possible, and certainly as a resource for all within the campaign.

That same week, despite the fact that the alliance had planned a media event involving everyone, the same person put out the media release without circulating any draft for approval, only mentioning their own community organisation (yes, the more 'powerful' one), and thereby making the rest of the alliance invisible. Furthermore, when someone in the wider alliance questioned this via email, quite soon after the media release went out, they were put in their place and told "we will discuss in the next meeting, not via email."

Now these incidents were a real challenge to myself in terms of self and practice. My felt response, like others, was one of anger and frustration, and the feeling of being excluded. People weren't seeking kudos, but some kind of honest reflection of the work. And also I felt bewildered: why this person's impulse towards control and exclusion?

A reflective practice in relation to self required several things that could help avoid reactive impulses. Firstly, it was crucial to avoid a knee-jerk reaction. Fortunately I could call someone else in the group and share my frustration privately, working on strategies for maintaining disciplined public behaviour. Secondly, I had to reflect on my own tendencies to avoid conflict. How would I, as occasional joint-chair of the group, process these feelings in a way that could nurture solidarity, but also not necessarily avoid conflict, particularly if conflict could be potentially generative? Thirdly, I needed an 'interpretation', to see into what was occurring, to try and make

sense of it. For example, I used the lens of traditions of 'political solidarity versus social solidarity' to make sense of how different people
were acting. Within this interpretation, the person described above
was possibly working from a political solidarity tradition, one of
command, discipline, control, exclusion of community, and a strong
clear single message. Whereas almost all the others in the alliance
were operating from a social solidarity tradition of association, co-
operation, sharing, open-ness, multiple messages. That interpretation helped me on one level to at least cognitively understand the
bewilderment I was experiencing. Of course, the interpretation could
be inaccurate, and would only be confirmed through many conversations and much listening. However, the point is that the interpretation helped me deal with initial bewilderment and frustration. It
helped me temper the feelings, which in turn helped to create an
emotional space to dance a 'responsive dance' that took into account
all the characters in this emergent story.

Another interpretation emerged from other conversations with
members of the alliance, people who couldn't understand the protagonist's constant need to grab media headlines and ensure 'their'
organisation was leading the pack. From a depth perspective, there
seemed to be not only the enacting of a political solidarity tradition,
but a possible psychological inflation. Unreflective needs for power
were fuelling a narcissistic energy in which the practice of our 'opponents' were also being mirrored in the way this person was operating — accusing government of being non-transparent, but doing
the same themselves!

I also was aware of 'ghosts' in the emergent story: another person
situated 'behind' or 'beside' the protagonist described above, directing things from the background, rarely attending the alliance meeting
and therefore never creating the possibilities of trust, relationships or

accountabilities to develop, but nevertheless exercising significant influence, even control. So the unfolding practice challenge was, or is, to navigate these feelings, agendas, and characters, keeping the eye on both the end game, the campaign goal, and the relationships that were being forged (or stretched and broken).

Finally, my practice also required the constant generation of empathic feelings, being conscious that a long-established community association was feeling threatened by the emergence of a bottom-up, organic community movement. No wonder it was hard for the protagonists above! I kept working hard to see the unfolding story from their point of view.

Being attentive to the unfolding story, its characters, and to myself as one character in that story certainly required careful practice, considered responsivity, along with some commitments: commitments to 'checking in' with others when I felt something, and ensuring that my feelings and responses resonated with others. It required the practice of regular conversations with several others, encouraging people to keep behaving well, to be inclusive, transparent and consultative, even when others were not. Finally, it required the practices of careful conflicting: bringing up some of the contentious issues in the campaign group meeting, usually punctuated by ensuring the group climate was conducive to caring for one another.

In conclusion

Community work practice and the self can benefit profoundly from a soul perspective. There is an orientation to interiority, to reflection, to careful conversation, to slowing down, to a focus not only on our doing but our being in the work. The story demonstrates the difficulty of community work practice: both the challenges of, in this case, joining and nurturing a community alliance, and the challenges to self – how to be effective, generative and skilled when things don't go so well, when the inevitable complexities arise from flawed people's efforts to (not) co-operate or co-opt. We, as community workers, are in the story, part of the fabric of practice, caught in myriad events that arise. There is no way of stepping outside the story and being separate and objective about it. A community worker cannot help but be taken along with the energies, the possibilities, but they're also trying not to just 'go with the flow'. Instead they're trying to insert a reflective pause, a space for soul, a place of careful practice and self-awareness.

HOW TO GET THERE

Go to the end of the path until you get to the gate.

Go through the gate and head straight out towards the horizon.

Keep going towards the horizon.

Sit down and have a rest every now and again.

But keep on going. Just keep on with it.

keep on going as far as you can. That's how you get there.

Leunig

Soul, spirituality and community work

D ISTINGUISHING SOUL from spirituality is not easy – for many of us, it would be impossible to do clearly. Priests, so-called tenderers of the spirit, have used the language of soul for centuries, so they certainly overlap. Yet the words *soul* and *spirituality* elicit different images and energies.

For me, these 'images' foreground the core of life, the centre, and then shift outwards, towards connection. Do the words of soul and spirituality bring up images in your own mind? Leonard Cohen provides a simple image, in which he says "real spirituality has its feet in the mud and its heart in heaven".[70] There's something rich in that image, combining the inner and outer, the upper and lower, the messy and clean.

While we've spoken of soul as being understood metaphorically and analytically, I'd suggest that the language of soul can best be understood *mythically*. 'Movement of the soul' occurs within us, or there is a 'nudge from the soul', and we find ourselves in dark places, or feeling high mountain energies, or entering into initiation or rupture

70   From Interview in Irish Times, 3rd November, 1995, by Joe Jackson.

(usually through illness, separation, death, redundancy). These experiences can only be truly understood through the language and images of myth. And we're not mythically literate: we don't read the great myths any more, and if we do, we don't know how to interpret them. Our culture is shallowing, becoming wintery, even losing its colours and turning to grey. Without myth, our culture lacks real story.

The ego resents myth, unable to be captured, resisting interpretation in any definitive way. Ego resents the shifts in life that mythological work invites and requires; ego moves against soul and myth, calling for a battle to end the bloodshed that fills myth (often painful endings in our lives); but soul enters the fray with a smile on her face. Soul is trickster energy, she is Loki, she sometimes wants to be Apollo and at other times Dionysius. She can be all over the place, and yet she knows where she is tugging us to go. She's alive sometimes, asleep at other times. We have to listen carefully to hear her.

We could never describe spirituality in this way. Spirituality would be understood more easily in terms of cultivating an inner life, or in the words of my friend Verne Harris, 'cultivating an inner life in the conviction that it connects to a being, a becoming, beyond the bounds of time and space'.[71] A liberating spirituality, maybe a soulful spirituality, one infused with myth, is about fostering connection, between self and self, self and other, self and nature. It is what philosophers Caputo and Derrida might think of as 'religion without religion'.[72] This also reminds us, as Martin Shaw points out, that religion can be the last defence against a religious experience.[73] There is a sense that people in pursuit of a spiritual life can easily ossify, and become rigid

71   Personal email exchange, 19.1.15
72   Caputo, J. D., *The Prayers and Tears of Jacques Derrida: Religion Without Religion* (Bloomington & Indianapolis: Indiana University Press, 1997).
73   Shaw, *A Branch in the Lightening Tree: Ecstatic Myth and the Grace in Wildness* ,141.

in their spiritual practice. It becomes a means of defence rather than a road to connection. It closes people down rather than opens them up. But it doesn't have to. I know many people alive in their spirituality, alive to their spiritual practices and deeply connected.

However, a soul and mythical orientation recognises, as per David Tacey's argument,[74] that despite the transition to a post-secular society, the modern ego is generally in the grip of an anti-spiritual enlightenment myth. Lacking a spiritual sensibility, many cling to a mechanistic worldview desperately still wanting control of society, of change processes, of economic development, of life — despite evidence to the contrary. Community workers are at risk of this same ego grip. At the same time many are now seeking a spiritual awakening, turning not to old religions, but to new spiritual practices. Some of these are liberating, enabling people to navigate a post-secular world with curiosity and compassion, surrendering the need to control, but holding on to a scientific sensibility alongside a renewed spiritual sensibility. Control has yielded to connection and compassion. Others are engaged in what can be described as more domesticating spiritual practices and movements, oriented towards fundamentalisms, fascisms and violence. Whatever direction they are leading us, the main point is that these spiritual energies are at play.

Dancing between the so-called spiritual and soul, I would suggest that a soul orientation offers a way for community workers to take seriously the undercurrents — the subtle, the sacred and spiritual — to ensure that practice is not driven by control. Without a lens or language to see these deeper mythological energies at work, and then work with them, accompany them carefully, ethically and strongly, a community worker's practice easily becomes disembodied and disconnected from the world of people. A soul orientation provides a

74 Tacey, *The Darkening Spirit: Jung, Spirituality, Religion.*

lens and language for community workers to re-socialise any spiritual energies into collective efforts filled with philosophy, conviviality, care, hospitality, the aesthetic and symbolic.

Instead of handing those spiritual energies over to the psychologists, where the symptoms of their manifestation are managed, denied, and drugged, community workers informed by a soul perspective can channel them into creative social processes. Instead of surrendering those spiritual energies to religious fundamentalists, who direct them into religious-political violence and social exclusion, community workers with a soul perspective offer a way to re-imagine the re-weaving of an animated, hospitable community, oriented towards connection, compassion and mythological imagining.

Community workers embracing a soul perspective will probably also bathe their feet in spiritual practices. Soul as we have conceived it is about animating energies within the physical body and body politic, and about that part of us that can discern the pull of those energies within and outside ourselves. At times such animated energies invite people and practitioners into action. However, at other times the invitation is into a space of reflection, of focused interior soul-work.

In a sense, then, a community worker who attends to soul and spirituality is attentive to both their own interior spiritual life and to the currents at work within the social field that can be understood as spiritual. Soul is the enabler of seeing, discerning, feeling the movements that are at work, and being able to work with them – being responsive and agile.

With a soul perspective that acknowledges spirituality, I love to celebrate particular stories of community practice. For example, the intentional community work practice of L'Arche communities draws on Catholic spirituality as a way of supporting community around people who live with profound disabilities. Another example, lived intentionally by a friend and colleague Dave Andrews, is that of community building work through inter-faith dialogue. Dave, accompanied by a young Muslim woman Nora, has been working for many years on such dialogue.

Having left the institutional church in the early 1990s, I have also endeavoured to still be disciplined in practices that can be construed as spiritually oriented. They are more in line with Tacey's 'spirituality from below', and include (mostly) daily meditation early in the morning. For me, meditation has a way of centering, building practices of awareness, and cultivating love towards others, generosity towards self, and solidity in intentional actions. At the heart of the practice is breathing. To make a conscious and mindful practice of breathing is to become aware of the pulsating and living processes that make us alive – the energy of soul. When all else is said and done, we can slow down, be present to the moment, pause, and breathe.

I love listening to Leonard Cohen, particularly with a glass of whisky while cooking Indian curry after a tough day at work. Cohen, a poet of profundity in lyrical beauty, helps me sit back, enjoy slowness, celebrate love and sensuality, and inhabit my mischievous self, my Loki, my trickster energy. His work affirms play, love, beautiful resistance – it's infused with a spiritual sensibility. Going to hear him live was like entering a holy place, bringing back old church-ghostly memories of the power of collective song.

I also cultivate the practice of regular walks in the wilderness, at least with one annual long walk. This ensures an encounter with nature in all its awe-inspiring beauty, power, complexity, intelligent sensibility and enfolding wildness. Moving literally from the town to the forest, the village to the mountain, also helps access different energies, available in places where I am rendered more vulnerable, where I have to be in the present. Have you ever walked through a forest with a pack and drifted mentally into other spaces? You'll trip over!

Often I go to the forest with the intention of thinking about or reflecting on life. Instead, I find that the rhythm of walking in forests, canyons and mountains draws me into the present, or more accurately into presence. I re-find a centre. Thinking or reflecting on life becomes meaningless in such spaces. I become aware of my small part in the large universe, alive for now, and soon to be dead, and a part of, rather than apart from, nature. It's interesting that when we drive from place to place, even beautiful places, we find ourselves stopping, catching glances, even 'trying' to soak in a landscape. But these processes fail to lead to *presence*. They are ever-fleeting moments. They lack depth and stillness. Presence requires walking, in which there is a slow arrival, a growing anticipation, a seeing from various angles, the body readying for the arrival, muscles and mind attentive to the destination. This anticipatory element seems to sum up the spiritual dimension of walking – the awareness of an approaching other, a caressing of senses as this other gets closer, and then an encounter with the other.

It's the soul within us, the gentle nudge that reminds us to attend to these spiritual practices. A soul perspective helps us notice these practices within others. An attentiveness to soul will sometimes also say "enough, it's time to get out on the streets again, or meet some friends at a bar, maybe even get a bit sloshed and sing karaoke." At the end of the day we don't find soul, it tends to find us. If we're lucky, it slowly sneaks up on us, inviting something different, and we hear that gentle voice. But for some of us it erupts into our lives through disruption, and offers Hades, mountains, valleys, forests, love, even hate.

A Little Duck

With a bit of luck
A duck
Will come into your life

When you are at the peak
Of your great powers.
And your achievement towers
like a smoking chimney stack
There·ll be a quack
And right there at your feet
A little duck will stand;
She will take you by the hand
And lead you
Like a child with no defence;
She will lead you
Into wisdom, joy and innocence.
That little duck.

We wish you luck.

Michael Leunig

Chapter Three

Soul of the World

N OT ONLY are people alive, animated by the life-force or living
energy, but so is the world, the cosmos. In Andrey Platonov's
classic novel *Soul*, the main character Chagataev puts it succinctly:
'Life itself is enough to earn you happiness! Our soul is in the world
now. And that's the only soul there is.'[75] To quote Rudolph Steiner, an
illustrious interpreter of Goethe, my soul and the great world are one.
Some authors, such as David Tacey and Thomas Moore, refer to a perspective that is aware of this animation as 're-enchanting the world'[76]
and others, such as James Hillman, as 'ensouling'.[77] It's this space and
practice of ensouling, or 're-enchanting the world' that I want to leap
into in this chapter. It feels like a leap, because it's mind-blowing,
breathtaking, paradigm-shifting stuff. It requires a great phenomenological leap into a different view and experience of the world.

75 Platanov, A, *Soul* (London: Vintage Books, 1999), 106.
76 Moore, T., *The Re-Enchantment of Everyday Life* (Sydney: Hodder & Stoughton,
    1996).
77 Hillman, J., *The thought of the heart and the soul of the world* (Connecticut:
    Spring Publications, 1992).

The idea of ensouling takes seriously the trace of thought within Carl Jung's opus, that views soul as a phenomenon beyond the individual psyche. The soul is not something in you, in your head, in your body. It's way beyond that. As David Tacey astutely argues, many contemporary readings of Jung have conveniently forgotten the trace of Jung's thought that sees soul as a cosmological phenomenon.[78]

James Hillman initiated the revival of this broader and deeper view of soul in the world, firstly in his seminal book *Re-Visioning Psychology*,[79] and then in his essay, 'Anima Mundi: The Return of the Soul to the World'.[80] Others have built on his work, such as the mercurial Thomas Moore, with his delightful book *The Enchantment of Everyday Life*.[81] A significant contribution is also made by one of the authors of *Liberation Psychologies*,[82] Mary Watkins, who wrote the influential essay 'Breaking the Vessels: Archetypal Psychology and the Restoration of Culture, Community, and Ecology'.[83] Here, soul is oriented towards a broader socio-cultural field, away from the individual psyche. It's in this broader orientation, a wider purview, that soul of the world connects with community work practice.

78 Tacey, *The Darkening Spirit: Jung, Spirituality, Religion.*
79 Hillman, J., *Re-Visioning Psychology* (New York: First Harper Colophon, 1975).
80 Hillman, J. "Anima Mundi: The Return of the Soul to the World," in Hillman, J., *The thought of the heart and the soul of the world* (Connecticut: Spring Publications, 1992).
81 Moore, *The Re-Enchantment of Everyday Life.*
82 Watkins, M. and Shulman, H., *Toward Psychologies of Liberation* (Basingstoke & New York: Palgrave Macmillan, 2008).
83 Watkins, M., "Breaking the Vessels: Archetypal Psychology and the Restoration of Culture, Community, and Ecology," in *Archetypal Psychologies: Reflections in honour of James Hillman edition*, Marlan, S. ed. (New Orleans, LA: Spring Books and Journals, 2008), 414-437.

Anima mundi and the world's suffering

Towards the end of his writing career James Hillman started to write about *anima mundi*, culture's soul. By this he was referring to the work of being attentive to the world's suffering, rather than our own individual suffering. As Moore states, reflecting on Hillman's work, "Our buildings are in pain, our governments are on the rocks, the arts are relegated to museums ...".[84] Clearly these issues are relevant to community workers, who are interested in public and cultural concerns, rather than private pain. Hillman focuses on what he sees as public pain, as manifestations of the world's suffering.

Within this frame, and linking to some of our previous discussions, soul cannot be reduced to the subjective, or captured by the ego or psyche. Soul has a life and a logic of its own: it is other, it's subtle. Therefore we can only get to know the soul of something if we enter into relationship with it. This is a challenge, because for most of us the only elements of life that we are conscious of in an everyday sense are ourselves and other people. We are used to *entering into relationship* with the self and other people; however, we perceive almost everything else as dead, or at least not alive enough to warrant a living relationship. This 'everything else' is treated as 'objects' of analysis rather than relational entities. A 'soul of the world' understanding could shift this latter objectifying and therefore deadening perception.

Intimacy with the world

Community work with soul includes practice oriented towards love of the world, that affirms people's individual inner worlds, but also this world of non-human living beings. A loving, 'soul of the world' orientation invites gentle, careful and imaginative engagement with

84   Moore, T., ed. *A Blue Fire: James Hillman* (Harper Perennial, 1989), 10.

these 'beings made alive' by a renewed intimacy with the world. We become intimate not only with other people — a norm within community work — but also with these other non-human dimensions of the world. And this intimacy is vital, because otherwise they are rendered dead to us by an imaginative frame that is deadening. Their life-force then takes on an autonomous life of its own. We end up with rampant economics, ugly architecture, and stuff that no-one needs.

A culture 'falling apart'

As an Australian I also write with a particular sensitivity to a moment in history where our culture could easily be construed as 'falling apart'. We live in a period of history experiencing profound dysfunction. People are disengaging from politics. We have developed a culture built around, or animated by, fear of the stranger (as I write, the 'other' are mainly Muslims, asylum-seekers and terrorists), and by corporate publicity and consumer-produced popular culture. At a cultural level Australia is broken — manifest in all sorts of endemic health conditions and a manic commitment to economic rationalism. There is a lack of quality conversation about political, economic, social, architectural, and ecological visions for life. Accompanying this is an epidemic of depression, anxiety and other 'mental health' issues. A holistic perspective is able to see connections between these issues.

Unfortunately it would seem that the 'falling apart' has not progressed to the point where most people are thinking more carefully about how to live. Within Australia there are only marginal spaces where Joanna Macy's so-called 'The Great Turning'[85] is occurring. There are glimpses, pockets maybe, of social, cultural, economic and ecological innovation, and yes, there are cracks in the 'great consumer

85   Macy, J. & Brown, M. Y., *Coming Back to Life: Practices to Reconnect Our Lives, Our World* (Gabriola Island, BC: New Society Publishers, 1998).

and producer culture' maintained by hegemonic interests. But at this stage the mainstream marches to the 'beat of the economic drum' and only the margins innovate.

When dreaming about our collective capacity to notice that 'things fall apart' culturally, it is also useful to reflect on how our life works at an individual level. For example, usually it is only when our individual lives fall apart – in depression, profound illness, or a major breakdown of relationship – that we start to imagine living from the perspective of soul, depth, other, hidden. We potentially become aware of our aloneness, deadened by a non-participatory worldview. Urged on by ego, vocation, career, and acquisitiveness, we stumble, trip up, but as soul awakens we potentially see things differently. What operates at the personal level is also true at a collective, social level. Community and culture will only be perceived from a soul perspective as we develop an awareness both of our own suffering and of its relation to our deep alienation from the world.

When people are in the middle of a fantasy of economic development, or the fantasy of technological salvation (remember the big dogmas), there is little chance of soul. People will not be open to the realms of the depths, the slow, the other; they will lack intimacy with the world. Like Icarus, they are flying high, far from the groundedness of the earth. I sense that this is why 'educational' attempts to shift people's perspective about the ecological crisis are largely ineffectual. They miss the mark. People are caught in a different and very powerful economic and technological fantasy. Desire is directed towards these economic and technological goals. The soul is colonised and captured by a particular dreamtime that is Every-where: materially-oriented culture. Only when people are themselves suffering, or truly attentive to someone else's suffering – when there is failure, or when a country, a culture, or a community feels broken, or cast aside — only then will people ask, 'What is going on?', or 'Who are we?' Only when we as a nation, a culture and community face the crises of:

- Mental illness and suicide as a symptom of a broken culture and community;
- The swamping of our culture by alcohol;
- Betrayal as a core practice of our political culture;
- Domestic violence as endemic;
- Our inability to sustain or mainstream any creative solutions in designing human-scale, or people-centred cities — after all, they're built for cars and designed mainly by property barons;
- Our over-reaching of planetary boundaries, whereby Australian consumption habits are quite literally destroying the world;
- Structural corruption, fed by a system of non-transparent political donations;
- The growing inequality in our society, with all the accompanying social cohesion pressures;

   — will we fully realise the depths of our current fantasy.

A manic society

There's also a profound technological fantasy, and I mention this because many people assume that crises will be solved by technology (remember the big dogmas discussed in the Introduction). Echoing Hillman, I would suggest that technology hasn't so much produced a society that is fast, but one that is *manic*. There is no pause in the frantic pace of life, and 24/7 culture is celebrated. People are immersed in manic conversations, without pause, learned or reinforced by phone culture where a pause leads to the fear that the other person is gone. So our manic communication becomes disembodied, lacking nuance and context. Manic culture is a way of avoiding soul orientation, which requires slowness, depth and interiority. When culture becomes manic, lacking interiority, it's almost impossible to even see the crises, let alone be intimate with the world's manifestations and consider new ways of being.

Inviting lostness

Hillman actually argues that 'lost-ness is a sign of soul'.[86] So in seeking an attention of community workers to soul of the world, I'm also inviting a certain lost-ness. We do not have to have all the answers. Many community workers nowadays are feeling the world's suffering, and are also re-awakening to their own suffering because they are learning to sense again. At this historical moment – one in which technocrats act with certainty and wilfulness, convinced that their technologies can solve all sorts of crises – soul will evoke a certain kind of humble weakness, as opposed to spiritedness. This is my intention in re-imagining community work; it's a different way to the ego-way, to wilfully construed interventions. But it should not be threatening to think of soulful community work as weak. Our cultural mania is a way of trying to get on top of our national crises, when we sense that 'things are falling apart'. Instead, we should fall into a national melancholy, embrace the grief within national crises, and in falling into them, notice, learn, slow down and attend to the subtle and latent energies that need care. We need to become sensitised to the symptoms and stay with them.

Also a soul perspective on community work, as per Hillman's depth psychology, is pluralist, in the sense that it does not restrict us to a single solution, or one narrative; it is multiple and plentiful. How

86   Hillman, *The thought of the heart and the soul of the world*, 17.

do we interpret the world's suffering, the loss of biodiversity, and human-made climate change? How do we interpret planners' manic obsessions with tall buildings? We need to approach these things with a phenomenological astuteness, sensitised to what is unfolding, and sensitised to our way of seeing, our fallacies in interpreting. Clearly we can't avoid eventually interpreting, but I'm trying to avoid the easy, non-reflective urge to quickly provide an interpretation, the jump to meaning which is the energy of the ego, that urgently wants to 'make sense' of something. A quick interpretation might satisfy the ego of the community worker, but it might also close down any openness to seeing, feeling or perceiving. A quick interpretation deadens a phenomenon by overlaying with abstracts and categories.

Places of oppression

Let's return to the soul of the world. Historically, people such as Freud or Jung attended to places of oppression within people's lives – their sex lives, or spiritual lives. But as Hillman says, 'where do we feel oppression today?'[87] We experience it at work, within public services, in the long hours spent commuting, and even longer hours working. So 'therapy' is needed to bring attention to these places of oppression.

Informed by a soul perspective, community workers need to bring an aesthetic sensibility to these community issues. In doing this it is easy to discern that many people today tend towards psychopathic, fundamentalist behaviour. By this I mean that people confuse the fantasy and the literal, and then act on their confusion. For example, people want happiness (a reasonable fantasy) but then conflate it with the economic, or with economic growth. Or happiness is conflated with beauty, and so people purchase breast enhancements.

87   Hillman, J., *Interviews* (Connecticut: Spring Publications, 1983), 125.

Metaphors become literal and the exterior colonises the interior. The world turns into a world of fundamentalists caught in a narrative that is psychopathic, literally destroying the planet. What gets lost is interiorisation, soul.

I think of the city where I live and work, Brisbane, whose culture poses a profound challenge to the kind of community work being proposed. Brisbane is obsessed with becoming a world city, depicted with tall buildings, splendid in iconic developments, fuelled by a property boom where property acquisition is the key to wealth. At the same time, people run and cycle along the river connected to their iPod, or iPhone, their bodies adapted to electronics, no longer at all sensitised to the sounds of their environments; the animal within them is lost. I also work at a 'sandstone' university obsessed with global rankings and quantitative output measures. So I am in this city and workplace, immersed in the syndromes of our times, the worlds suffering all around me, as we consume, build, dig, destroy, all for a fantasy of 'development'. Our lives mirror the myth of Icarus, flying higher and higher, totally unaware of our melting waxed wings. And we will fall, opening up the soul space.

In a sense our psychological concretism, caught up in the myth of development, is also caught in a soul-less space, because everything is dead except the ego. As already said, animals, buildings, things, and even economics, are rendered dead, soul-less, of not having their own life. As soul-less and lifeless, it is easy to manipulate them, instead of holding them in respect and participating in their life. 'Soul of the world' invites a perspective of seeing soul in everything again, a post-secular awareness in all things. I'm not talking about a return to primitive animism, but about an aesthetic, sensual engagement which requires us to re-animate the public concerns of community work with our imaginative faculties.

Care, not cure

As already mentioned, a key insight within a soul perspective is that to remove symptoms too quickly is to cure away soul. In fact from a depth perspective, symptoms such as domestic or family violence, degenerative social conflict, and myriad social problems, are sure indicators that something is amiss. However, the response is not cure, in the sense of removing the violence, conflict or social problems, but welcome care. A response that takes the soul of the world seriously invites an imaginative and caring response to such symptoms. In fact, in the same way that for individuals, painful symptoms might herald new ways of how to be, live, and love, painful societal symptoms related to the world's suffering also demand a different way of being, living and loving. Such awareness demands a different way of building cities, planning for our streets and open spaces, curating artistic expression and endeavours, responding to graffiti, and caring for rivers, wetlands, and reefs.

Attending to current symptoms of social problems and oppression with a caring paradigm requires discernment, patience, waiting, pausing, and listening. One useful insight, gained from reflecting on Hillman's work around suicide, is that soul's meaning "is best given by context".[88] By this Hillman is referring to the notion that behaviour is understandable because it has an inside meaning.[89] There is a sense that just as an individual's behaviour has a particularity, and can only be understood through 'inside meaning', a community is also experiencing *its own* suffering and there is a need to make meaning of it 'from the inside', so to speak. A soul perspective eschews a one-size-fits-all blueprint to solving social problems within

88 Hillman, J., *Suicide and the Soul* (Connecticut: Spring Publications, 1964), 44-45.
89 Ibid.

community. Social problems, though found in similar form across the whole of society, have a particular story within each community. That's not to say there are not linkages between communities and the unfolding stories within each community, nor that people in different places cannot learn from one another, and even at times work collaboratively. It's simply to say that the starting point of practice is slow and careful work with the particular – to do the patient work of listening and discerning within a particular community or group.

As an example, let's think about our fantasies of 'redemptive violence', that is, the myth that we can deal with someone or something we don't like by repression or violence. Policy makers and strategists don't like terrorist action, so they start a 'war on terror'; yet the evidence seems to indicate that this war has not reduced the number of so-called terrorists. Similarly with the 'war on drugs' mentality, or myth, that plays out in many domains of public and private life. Communities don't like young people doing graffiti, so they start the equivalent of a war on graffiti. Instead, a soul perspective invites an engagement with the particularity of a place, with its own manifestation of drugs, graffiti, family fragmentation, and unemployment. Such deep engagement provides a space for stories and nuanced analyses to unfold. Links can also be made between particular places and a broader story – and a deeper meaning would arise. For example, and again referring to young people's graffiti, rather than identifying it as vandalism and criminalising such actions, a soul perspective would ask questions such as: Do young people have a voice? Where can they express themselves publicly in artistic endeavours? What kinds of marginalisation are young people experiencing in our society? Even asking such questions invites a plurality of interpretations about the manifest symptom (graffiti) and opens possibilities for community work.

The beauty of a soulful approach to working with community issues, infused with imagination and participatory and phenomenological views, is that community represents in many ways a pluralistic set of interpretations grounded in the particular of a locality or place. This is especially so if a community worker can hold a space for conversations that include the other and the different, the subtle and the latent energies and ideas. Multiple interpretations of the presenting social symptom provide fertile ground for various responses.

A framework of community practice

Mary Watkins' practices of community work, drawing on Hillman's *opus,* offer a useful framework that takes soul of the world seriously. The framework can be understood as offering signposts that ground a phenomenological approach to community work with soul. Each signpost builds on the other, guiding a community workers engagement into working with cultural, ecological and social phenomena.

Notitia

Watkins explores how Hillman's answer to her question, 'How are [we]... to enter into the fray of community and ecological work?'[90] focuses on the practice of 'noticing', or what he called *notitia*. There is the need to keep looking, listening, and noticing, and *keep doing it more*. Watkins explains how Hillman prioritises sight over feeling at the early stage of working with any phenomenon, arguing that practitioners need to begin with noticing, paying attention to the specifics relevant to the singular event, moment, or place. This noticing needs "the gift of careful attention that is sustained, patient, subtly attuned to images and metaphors, tracking both hidden meanings and sur-

90 Watkins, "Breaking the Vessels", 6.

face presentations".[91] Linking to a phenomenological approach, such as articulated by Allan Kaplan,[92] this requires "open pathways to the depth of a phenomenon".[93] For Hillman, such work is countercultural, rejecting the hyperactivity of modern culture and its expectation of a quick response.

As I explained in *Dialogical Community Development*, this noticing requires the capacity to let go of immediate or pre-determined agendas and analyses, and to be open to what might be at play in any social or ecological situation — to be open to what might be 'becoming'. Watkins argues that our disposition needs to be of 'apprenticeship',[94] with an 'openness to being tutored' by the social phenomenon. In my experience this is not easy work. Many of us are quick to leap to an interpretation; we do what Otto Scharmer calls 'downloading'[95] and draw on past experiences that give us an answer to the current experience. In drawing on the past, we become unable to see within the present and see possible futures. Many of us are resistant to seeing — it's a discipline or habit we have not cultivated. For example, we see the form of a tree, and quickly in our mind it's abstracted as 'tree' and categorised. We no longer see the particularity of that tree. We don't experience it in all its beauty, texture, decay, growth, and colour. We're like Ronald Reagan saying, "If you've seen one redwood, you've seen them all".[96] We don't get intimate with the tree — we don't notice it! This is just as true of social situations. Noticing therefore requires a whole new habituation and discipline, to stop quickly drawing on the past, to avoid abstracting and categorising, and instead to look, listen, observe, ask ...

91 Ibid., 7.
92 Kaplan, *Development Practitioners and Social Process: Artists of the Invisible.*
93 Watkins, "Breaking the Vessels", 7.
94 Ibid., 7.
95 Scharmer & Kaufer, *Leading from the Emergent Future.*
96 Bly, *Iron John,* 231.

In tune with ugliness and beauty

According to Hillman and Watkins, once we have patiently and carefully noticed what is going on in culture, community, and ecological processes, we become attuned to ugliness and beauty. In noticing, and paying deep attention, new and deep emotions strike us; for Hillman this aesthetic response is linked to the ethical: "it does not replace the ethical, but it gives sensate images that direct our longings towards ideals, visions that we can become seduced by".[97] Hillman argues that we have repressed our aesthetic involvement in the world, numbing our ability to feel or see beauty and ugliness. That repression tends to undermine our capacities to see or feel the connections between our personal depression and other dimensions of life, the *polis* or politics. To reconnect the personal and political is to recognise that our misery is not only a result of our intra- or interpersonal relations. As Hillman states, "beauty evokes love".[98] Watkins adds, "an aesthetic response fuels protest".[99]

Depression and melancholy

Watkins also explains how "... depression must not be seen only as a result of personal history and problems, but that it is a response to a world shared with others".[100] However I suggest we re-orient this element of the practice framework away from depression and towards melancholy, recognising that depression is often about a loss of vitality, the life-force, whereas melancholy is about grief, but still with an energy to work with, or accompany the grief.[101] Within this

---

97 Watkins, "Breaking the Vessels", 10.
98 Hillman, J., "Aesthetic Response as Political Action," in *City and Soul*, ed. Leaver, R. J. (2006), 143.
99 Watkins, "Breaking the Vessels", 10.
100 Ibid., 10.
101 I am indebted to a conversation with Mark Creyton to understand the difference between the two, with Mark's inspiration being the need to re-orient away from the language of depression and more towards melancholy.

framing, as we widen our attention, we discover that the hoarding of the idea of soul within self, and not the world, has served a defensive function, protecting us from the tragedies and travesties in our midst.[102] Melancholy is grief at work, an inevitable part of realising that things are 'falling apart', and in turn, awareness of such grief can enable us to attend to the deeper feelings that we feel about the world as it is being made. In turn we can re-make the world to a different tune.

Multiplicity

Within archetypal psychology, our psyche is imagined pluralistically, in the sense that within our psyches there are often contradictory and paradoxical voices. I should add that there is often a domineering ego trying to silence these many voices. The ego wants control, domination and a unified story. But the soul wants multiplicity and complexity. Within archetypal theory, where the multiplicity of the psyche is repressed, it voices itself through symptoms and possibly pathology. The responsive practice of the therapist is to 'bracket' the domineering ego and make space for un-listened to and or silenced voices. They are often heard at the margins, having been persistently marginalised.

This viewpoint and practice of psychology has its parallel in community and cultural practice. Our society tends to privilege and amplify strong domineering voices. Culture is popularised and commodified, producing simplistic messages and modes of being. Other marginal voices and cultural practices are repressed. For example, as Martin Shaw has explained, the culture of wildness or wilderness is one example of repressed, almost lost, culture. A community worker bringing an archetypal frame to their practice is required to listen in a much broader way than the norm, searching for multiple possible interpre-

102 Watkins, "Breaking the Vessels", 10.

tations, and more specifically as per the commitments of community work, the "neglected, unheard, repressed and denied viewpoints".[103]

Dialogue

Listening to new perspectives, such as those offered from the margins, requires a capacity for dialogue. A soul perspective almost always moves beyond one voice, one analysis. Dialogue is crucial in working with the multiple perspectives that bring a more soulful understanding of a social situation: one of depth, holistic awareness, and responding to subtle, latent energies. Often such dialogue requires the creation of what can be understood as sacred spaces, often thought of within community work as Circle Work, or within indigenous practice as Yarning Circles.

From the perspective of 'soul of the world', we also need to create dialogical spaces to engage more broadly around ecological, cultural and community issues. Mary Watkins shares a story of urban planners who realised how few people were actually involved in city planning processes. They started to think about questions such as: how could a city come alive to its population if it didn't represent more of the dreams of the people who live there? Similarly, how can we care for a coral reef if we do not hear the voices of people, animals and other creatures, whose lives are connected to the reef? An ensouled perspective engages with a broader constituency than would normally be considered.

Seeing through

Watkins reminds us of Hillman's assertion that "we are always in the embrace of an idea".[104] A soul perspective requires a wrestling

103 Ibid.,13.
104 Ibid., 17.

with the ideas we have embraced, acknowledging their historical and cultural roots. A community work approach that takes seriously 'soul of the world' requires us to wrestle with our whole worldview. For example, who or what do we include in dialogue when considering a social or community problem? Are we excluding a perceived enemy or opponent? Our ideas are inevitably full of myth and fantasy, and 'seeing through' requires a meditative engagement with these mythological and fantasy-bearing elements. Without this wrestling, or engagement, our ideas, or the ideas of others, are accepted as natural and inevitable. They become hegemonic. We shut out space that should be open to possible dissent and disruption.

The practice of seeing through ideas should liberate community workers to be creative with ideas rather than victims to them. In understanding ideas historically and culturally, we can play with them, shift perspective, and create new ideas.

The imaginal

At the heart of a community practice that takes 'soul of the world' seriously, is an invitation to honour images. This requires a reversal of the urge to subjectivity (to reflect on how *we feel* as a response to something). The challenge is to hold off that urge, and instead attend to images of the world as presented through a personal story of experience, or an unfolding story of what is going on in a community: to see the images arising, and expand and deepen them through artwork, theatre, and other forms of presenting the story. New textures and granularity can be discerned. The story thickens, becomes richer. Ultimately the narrative thread, an 'interpretation' of what is seen and what could be done, then becomes more accurate. The community action is more powerful, infused with soul.

Reflection and action

In *Revisioning Psychology,* James Hillman explains that

> Ideas allow us to envision, and by means of vision we can know...
> But when an insight or idea has sunk in, practice visibly changes.
> The idea has opened the eye of the soul. By seeing differently, we
> do differently. Then 'how' is implicitly taken care of.[105]

The words that strike me here are "when an idea or insight has sunk in", again a manifestation of a soul movement − not to be stuck within an intellectual understanding of an idea, but to let it 'sink in', to become a part of us. Here is the transformational space, the 'aha!' experience, the mercurial moment. Reflection and action, as living processes of searching for truth, the essence of re-search, are what enable such sinking processes to occur. Depth is the result. We need to recognise that both reflection and action are activities, and in their polarity, there is currently too much emphasis on action (remember the lack of interiority). For Hillman, bringing these together in a more living, dynamic relationship leads to the bringing of 'soul into action, and action into soul'.[106] Essentially a soul perspective invites many of the practices outlined above into social activism − noticing, reflecting, seeing through, and so forth. Bringing those into social activism enables the emergence of a more powerful social praxis that enlivens the classical Freirian praxis of reflection and action. For Watkins the real potential is the bringing together of both Freire's action and reflection *and* love and observation (seeing through). Hillman's aesthetic orientation can only add to Freire's radical liberatory praxis.

105 Hillman, *Re-Visioning Psychology,* 121-122.
106 Watkins, "Breaking the Vessels", 19.

Conclusion

Each of us has to respond to the soul of the world, and the manifestation of that soul within us. That response will be a unique pathway, evoked by a sensitivity to the world's calling. Maybe the pathway will emerge as a response to the nudges or images of dreamwork,[107] or through a serendipitous meeting with someone that opens up a doorway to social involvement. Maybe it's attending a workshop that gives you a glimpse of a new world, or the result of unbidden feelings of discontent with what one is already doing. The point is that we each need to respond to the unique call, and the unique way in which that call manifests itself. The world yearns for witness, for participation, for coming alive; or more accurately, the world within us yearns to make the world alive, to participate in a new, intimate, living way. Are we listening?

In this same way, communities are suffering – in their economic approach, their transport systems, their manic addiction to work or consumer-oriented entertainment. These communities also have symptoms of pain, calling towards soul. It could be a suicide that triggers some awakening, or simply an overwhelming sense amongst a particular group that something is 'falling apart'. Conversations are then triggered, dialogue and analysis unfold, with deep listening that creates an intimacy within community and with the 'object of concern', holding the images of what is wrong, or what is offered as a way forward. Interpretations and narrative threads are distilled. Powerful action can emerge. So, again, are we listening and seeing?

---

107 See the delightful story recounted by Stephen Aizenstat about a group of young people connecting their depressions, dreams and social action around ecological crises, in Aizenstat, S., "Fragility of the World's Dream," in *Eranos Yearbook 2009-2011: Love on a Fragile Thread,* eds. Merlini, F., et al. (Daimon Verlag, 2012).

Poor old lonely mother earth
Is very, very sad,
She had a bomb put in her heart
By people who were mad;
She held them and she fed them;
She taught them to be free.
They put a bomb inside her heart
And whispered, "C'est la vie"

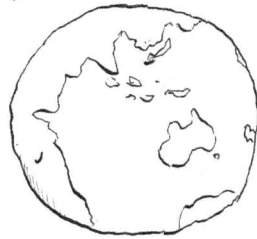

Leunig

Soul and resistances

F OR MANY PEOPLE, the concept of soul would evoke ideas that I have mentioned in previous chapters: ideas such as care, attention, mindfulness and spirituality. They infer a quality of being and living that *feels* soulful. Few people would associate soul with resistance. However, that is what I propose to explore in this interlude, addressing a 'tradition' of thinking about soul that is more critical of the socio-political, economic, aesthetic and technological forces that shape our being. To be critical of those forces is to invite resistance.

As we considered in the Introduction, soul is not only about energies within the body or the cosmos as force, but also about an energy field. Field refers to the notion that energies within us are not constructed by some 'essence' (remember I avoid the notion of soul as essence), but are instead constructed or shaped by what we are immersed within. These is a sense in which our habits of life, which in many ways reflect the energies within us, are in fact shaped by a broader social field. For example, if we have a habit of going to shopping malls, this habit is probably linked to the social field of mass publicity seducing us to go there.

Trying to understand that broader social field requires due attention if people are to live with some awareness of the forces shaping
their lives. Often the 'gentle nudge of the soul' clashes with the field
we are immersed in, shaping the soul, even colonising it. If that clash
becomes untenable, many of us end up sick, ill, or depressed. If the
clash is resolved through repeatedly ignoring the gentle nudge of the
soul, we become something other than our Great Self. In mythical
terms, the King is no longer at the head of Arthur's Round Table; we
are no longer the author of our own story. It becomes important to
understand the field that shapes soul.

Our understanding can begin with 'Bifo' Beradi,[108] an Italian writer whose critical theory focuses on understanding contemporary cap-
italism and its particular restructuring of the workplace. Within this
analytical lineage, he argues that since the 1970s, at least within
advanced capitalist economies, work has been transformed for many
as a place of cognitive labour, as people use their minds at work more
than their bodies. It is within this space of cognitive labour that desire,
creativity and imagination are most manifest. It is where most people
love to be, in contrast to the time prior to the 1970s, when most people wanted to work less, as work was mainly mechanical labour. In
Better than Sex: How a whole generation got hooked on work, Helen
Trinca and Catherine Fox explain how for many people "suddenly
it's fine to admit that work means a lot to us, that we like our jobs,
that we sometimes feel more complete and integrated at work than
in our private lives",[109] and even add some juicy detail, that maybe
"work life is more fulfilling, empowering, consistent and controllable
than their sex lives".[110] In writing about soul, numerous authors see

---

108 Beradi, *The Soul at Work: From Alienation to Autonomy.*
109 Trinca, H. & Fox, C., *Better than Sex: How a whole generation got hooked on
     sex* (NSW, Australia: Random House Australia, 2004). 4.
110 Ibid., 3.

the real benefits of this experience of work, arguing that at last "we can be ourselves, bringing our creativity into the workplace".[111] In a sense, then, people are now at their most creative, intelligent selves at work, and therefore they want to spend more time there.

As a result, people's identities and energies are constructed less from community, or the social fabric of society, than from the 'social factory' where they are employed. For many, work becomes their community. However, from a critical perspective this creative and imaginative work is contextualised by a competitive neoliberal capitalist economic system, which creates failure (after all it is impossible for everyone to win in a competitive space), stress (people become tired of creating, of constantly making themselves, of competing), ultimately manifest in anxiety, panic and depression. Bifo argues that the soul has been colonised[112] by this kind of modern cognitive labour in the social factory, and that furthermore, 'something in the collective soul has seized up'.[113] For Bifo, soul, as gravity of the body, takes people into these seized, panicked, depressed places as a gift, inviting reconsideration of how they might want to live and work.

With such an analysis in mind, a soul perspective on community work also considers, in dialogue with the likes of Bifo, how to recreate autonomous and strategic sites of work, action and community that offer an alternative to the current structure of neoliberal capitalist enterprise. Soul signifies an aesthetic response to orthodox notions of contemporary work, and a call to reorient sensuality and vitality away from the social factory of work and towards re-weaving the social fabric of community – a new 'ecology of late capi-

111 Whyte, D., *The Heart Aroused* (London, UK: Industrial Society, 2002).
112 Beradi, *The Soul at Work: From Alienation to Autonomy*, 14.
113 Ibid., 10.

talism' and radical reform.[114] This in turn requires a re-imagining of wealth consumption, letting go of the anxiety-driven need to earn more money and secure more economic wealth. Connolly argues that

> today perhaps the initial target should be on constituting estab-
> lished patterns of consumption by a combination of direct citizen
> action in consumption choices... the organization of local collec-
> tives to modify consumption practices, and social movements to
> reconstitute the current state- and market-supported infrastructure
> of consumption.[115]

It is ultimately a call for courage in working out how to do good work in our society, and consume in a different way, dissociated from the narcissistic, fear-inducing, competitive urges inbuilt within most capitalist workplaces. Such a perspective leads to the insight that community work informed by the perspective of soul *might* actually be more a practice and movement of the affluent, than the so-called poor. While the poor are often (importantly, not always) desperate-ly trying to climb the ladder of wealth, the already wealthy, struck down by collective panic, anxiety and depression, are seeking for 'something other'. Energies against development, and anti-capitalist practice, might well find a groundswell amongst the middle classes wanting to downsize. This is not to say that the so-called poor are not living with soul; many are, as they practice a slow rhythmic life, filled with ritual, hospitality, story, care and harmony.

This analytical framework raises fundamental questions: how does each person choose to live and work, or how might each of us indi-vidually, then collectively, re-imagine our freedom? Here Nicholas

114 Connolly, W., *The Fragility of Things: Self-Organising, Processes, Neoliberal Fantasies, and Democratic Activism* (Durham & London: Duke University Press, 2013), 37.
115 Ibid., 38.

Rose's works, *Governing the Soul*[116] and *Powers of Freedom*,[117] offer
some useful frames of thinking.

Rose argues that within most modern societies there is little that
we share — we don't share identity or an essence (as Australians, for
example). What we do share is our status as subjects of government.
Basically, most of the time, we all do what we're told. And we do this
because we are subjects of "regimes that act upon our conduct in the
proclaimed interest of our individual and collective well-bring".[118]
That is, we tend to align our own interests with those who govern
us. However, Rose argues that, "to the extent that we are governed
in our own name, we have a right to contest....",[119] in fact, we have a
responsibility to contest. Without this contestation, democracy is in
deep trouble.

To counter a troubling trend towards non-contestation, Rose offers an 'ethic of vitalism', a political disposition that yearns for an
'active art of living'. This political vitalism is in favour of the "ob-
stinate, stubborn and indomitable will to live, and of the conditions
that make possible the challenge to existing modes of life and the
creation of new modes of existence".[120] Rose is particularly concerned
that modes of life tend to be shaped by a way of thinking that is too
focused on morality at the expense of ethics. The end of the continuum that represents morality is one in which life options become codified as natural, given, uncontestable, normal, pro-social — I would
say, a frame without soul, with little space or energy for movements
within or without. At the other end, understood as the 'ethical pole',

116 Rose, N., *Governing the Soul: The shaping of the private self* (London & New
     York: Free Association Books, 1989).
117 Rose, N., *Powers of Freedom: Reframing Political Thought* (Cambridge, UK:
     Cambridge University Press, 1999).
118 Ibid., 284.
119 Ibid., 284.
120 Ibid., 283.

there is a radical openness, resisting codified versions of 'normal and uncontestable ways of being'. He sees this end of the continuum represented by a 'politics whose ethos is reluctance to govern too much, that minimises codification and maximises debate'. Furthermore it's a way of being

> that seeks to increase opportunities for each individual to construct and transform his or her own forms of life, that validates diverse ethical criteria and encourages all to develop and refine their practice and experimental arts of existence.[121]

In a sense soul requires that we cultivate particular 'arts of living'. The argument is that we can't afford, as citizens, to fall into a state of passivity. Soul, as the body energised, requires a vital engagement with politics and this art of living. There is recognition that every kind or style of government implies a way of living, a form of life, and the question remains as to whether people are still engaged in discerning the possibilities and limits within the current form. Are people alive to their formation, and discerning possibilities? Has our imaginative literacy shrunk to the point of 'there is no alternative' (TINA), and have we become zombies? An ethic of vitalism can inform a soul perspective on community practice, inviting people to be in conversation as groups, or as collectives, about their way of life and the way they are governed.

It is useful to ground the practice of ethical vitalism in soulful community work. People, in relationship with others, need to resist hegemonic tendencies of neoliberal corporate culture to portray its greed as 'common sense'. Soulful community work offers both the *soul dimension* and *community dimension* to this process of resisting. The soul dimension invites a depth analysis of what shapes how we

121 Ibid., 193.

live. Only in unmasking the normal, the everyday common sense, can we penetrate the ideology of choice that underpins modern post-capitalist society.[122] Desire is produced, via mass media, advertising, and consumer ideology. Choice, fuelled by desire, without any awareness of what shapes that desire, is delusional. Freedom, linked to resistances, requires a renewed depth awareness and analysis.

The community dimension insists that this cannot be done alone. Resistances and artful living flourish when people *together* do the soul-depth analysis. Historically, community workers have often thought of this as conscientisation – people becoming aware about, or literate about, the word and world, widening their imaginative literacy. Such processes of conscientisation allow people to be more aware of ways of being and living, consuming and acquiring. We are looking for ways to nurture one another, as community, in vital flourishing.

This soul reflection on resistance has focused on the crucial part post-industrial capitalist economies play in shaping the way we live. In turn we have considered how we might reverse the colonisation of the soul by workplaces, consumption habits and forms of governance that diminish contestation. Refusing to 'be what we've become', resistance insists in putting our energies back into reweaving the social fabric of community, whilst reshaping how we consume and accumulate wealth, with recognition that such resistance cannot be achieved alone. Community has a significant role in supporting people in conversations about an art of living that affirms contestation and flourishing. *Viva la revolución*!

122 Salecl, R., *Choice* (London, UK: Profile Books, 2010).

GUNK

He woke up completely covered with gunk.

All around him, everything in the room was covered with gunk.

And outside too; the streets, the houses, the entire city seemed to be covered with gunk!

People everywhere were smothered with it; **gunk had worked** its way into, onto EVERYTHING and EVERYONE.

How tired, heavy and dull it made the world. Nothing sparkled any more; nothing moved freely.

What was it? What was this GUNK? What was it composed of, where did it come from and what was to be done about it?
Why were so many people PROMOTING it?

leunig

Chapter Four

Soul-force

A BOOK ON SOUL and community work can hardly ignore the significance of Mahatma Gandhi's idea of *satyagraha,* or soul-force. It's an idea that orients towards the implications of soul for collective nonviolent social action and resistance, as we explored in the Interlude. If soul of the world takes community workers towards an intimacy with the world, then soul-force takes us into the space of courage, truth, love and social action.

Gandhi's soul-force was part of his experiment with life and politics that emphasised the importance of truth and love, words not usually associated with politics. A political program infused with truth and love is apt to be full of soul!

There are several reasons for taking Gandhi as a starting point, although it is also fruitful to engage with Rabindranath Tagore, as a balance to the rather austere political program of Gandhi, that can easily be construed as soul-less. Firstly, in my early days as a community worker I was deeply influenced by the teachings of Gandhi, particularly as interpreted by Dave Andrews and Anthony Kelly. They inducted me into what can be thought of as a social-reconstruction tradition of community work, informed by ideas and practices such as nonviolence, intentional community, civil disobedience, the integration of the personal and political, the importance of justice for the poorest of the poor, creative resistances, and simplicity. Secondly, Gandhi was known as Mahatma or Great Soul — an example to many people of how to live and work, and how to organise for social change and much besides. Finally, he developed the notion of soul-force, a way of anchoring truth and force together in ways that integrated the strategic, moral and spiritual. Here was a vision for life, most easily accessed through a brief consideration of his core ideas:

- Nonviolence as a way of life, not only as a tactic in freedom struggles;
- The philosophy of *sarvodaya*, which is a deep commitment to the well-being of all;
- The politics of *swaraj*, with a focus on self-rule (ruling of our self as opposed to ruling over others) and self-organisation — which needs to be understood not only as an organising principle related to governance, but also a personal and spiritual practice of taking full responsibility for self;
- The economics of *swadeshi*, with a commitment to local economic self-reliance. This entails the dignity of labour, giving priority to human-scale economies and appropriate technology.

A key contemporary of Gandhi, Tagore also spent significant time reflecting on the links between love and force.[123] Barry Hill quotes Tagore's pertinent words, "when love and force do not go together, then love is mere weakness and force brutal."[124] For Tagore, such coming together is also reflected in his commitment to bringing the

---

123 Hill, *Peacemongers*, 58.
124 Ibid., 58.

social and soul together, holding an aesthetic and social-political sensibility within a holistic frame. And crucially, within this holistic frame there is a somewhat antagonistic dialogue between Gandhi and Tagore which is indicative of some misgivings about Gandhi's soul-force. For Tagore, Gandhi's interpretations of 'life's training was different' to his own, with Gandhi's focus being 'the eradication of life's joy', and his own being 'the purification of life's joy.'[125] For Tagore there should be no aesthetic antagonism to social life itself – in fact, the hope was harmony. He explains in his typically beautiful words:

> [Life] was like our musical instrument *tambura* whose duty is to supply the fundamental notes to the music to save it from going astray into discordance. It believed in *anadam,* the music of the soul, and its own simplicity was not to kill it but to guide it.[126]

Tagore's disagreement with Gandhi is that Gandhi's struggle becomes *primarily* a struggle 'against something' rather than 'for something'. In contrast Tagore is arguing *for life*, for a deeper vision of how to live, and sees nonviolent action as it was being deployed by Gandhi as essentially anti-life. While not necessarily agreeing with Tagore, my ideas resonate with Tagore's work, recognising that in many ways his philosophy of life and learning is more attuned to my reflections on soul. Like Allan Ginsberg's poetic reflections on Moloch,[127] Tagore saw that 'today the human soul is lying captive in the dungeon of the Great Machine',[128] and he wanted people to rediscover a life-giving vision of love, art, philosophy, conviviality, play, joy, dance, and music.

125 Ibid., 144.
126 Ibid., 144.
127 Allan Ginsberg refers to Moloch in his famous poem *Howl*.
128 Hill, *Peacemongers*, 163.

Even in Tagore's lifetime, people were questioning whether it was possible at the same time to be socially radical and to talk of soul. Later in his life Tagore noted that 'I have not convinced a single sceptic that he has a soul, or that moral beauty has greater value than material power.'[129] In a sense, while Gandhi drifted towards social action and asceticism, Tagore was able to hold a view of the world that was both socially revolutionary and also more poetic, more philosophical, more sensual and embodied, characterised by 'the clean and radiant fires of individual expression.'[130] Tagore wanted us to cultivate a love for something! In many ways our exploration of soul, with its celebration of culture, aesthetics, vitality, and imagination, is reaching for something new – a newness of quality, of being, of practice in the world. In the tradition of Tagore it is "for hope in all that was 'creative', in 'pathmaking,' in 'wakefulness at daybreak' ... and in the 'harmonies' of life."[131] Somehow I'd like to walk a middle path, articulating some of the relevance of Gandhi's soul-force but also taking into account the poetic sensibility of Tagore.

But you might be asking: why do we need soul-force at this historical moment, where many people feel that life is 'all right'? For 40 years the 'neoliberal project' has promoted a successful program of action against the kinds of values and images that soulful community work tries to promote. That project has cultivated a worldview, a cultural narrative that is about the individual, about survival of the strongest and greediest; it's been about the free market and selling off of public assets. It's been *against* collective action, mutualism, love, truth and co-operative efforts; it's been *for* McMansions, four-wheel drives, cheap air-travel, fossil fuel, and air-conditioning

129 Ibid., 166.
130 cited in Hill, *Peacemongers,* 219.
131 Ibid., 162.

for all. It's been for the privatisation of medical care and education, and for speculative investment in multiple homes, while the poor are left to fend for themselves with ever-increasing rents. Ultimately, as discussed by both Richard Sennett[132] and Anne Mann,[133] we've very successfully created and nurtured a narcissistic culture.

However, analysis also requires a more careful understanding of the forces at work that need both resistance *against* neoliberal hegemonic forces and collective action *for* a new socially-oriented political economy. For example, as sociologists Zygmunt Bauman and Carlo Bordoni remind us, most people no longer feel as though their lives are managed, controlled, or regulated by state action; on the contrary, there has been a powerful shift from regulation to seduction.[134] The state, in alignment with corporations, invokes desire as its main means of control, via ever-present public relations machines and advertising. The ultimate social contract is no longer between state and citizen, but between commodity producer and consumer. So resistance is tricky – it's not necessarily about the kind of politics conventionally advocated by activist practitioners.

Governments also create and perpetuate a 'state of crisis', focused usually on economic or security threats, that positions people to think about *their own* individual or family survival. When people are unsure about the future, they clamour for more for themselves. They hunker down and hold onto what they have. It's 'us' or 'me' versus 'them' or 'you'. Social solidarities and love for the earth are undone in the quest for holding onto what are perceived to be limited resources.

132 Sennett, R., *Together: The Rituals, Pleasures and Politics of Cooperation* (London & New York: Penguin Press Group, 2012).
133 Manne, *The Life of I: The New Culture of Narcissism.*
134 Bauman, Z. & Bordoni, C., *State of Crisis* (Cambridge: Polity Press, 2014), 48. This is not necessarily true for the many people living under the fear of dictatorships and military regimes.

This uncertainty and 'holding on' creates the conditions for the state to then manage people's emotions, which is understood within sociological literature as 'therapy culture'.[135] This is not to say that there is not a crisis upon us; but it is a different kind of crisis to that which governments try to create. I've argued that the soul of the world is suffering, and people need to see and feel the deep ecological and cultural crisis that is manifest in that suffering, and in turn feel their own suffering. Our political leaders simply focus on the wrong crises.

This kind of analysis provides interesting food for thought about where action can be directed. How does the anchoring of truth with force engage with these kinds of propositions about the direction and development of our society? Clearly there are individual responses, but 'community' has a place in any kind of 'fight-back' for a society oriented more towards social justice, social solidarities, social democracy and ultimately soul. We have explored many ideas – conversation, philosophy, an ethic of vitality, conviviality, and beautiful resistances in consumption habits, among others. And it should be said that if 40 years of the neoliberal project has created the narcissistic individual, has fragmented social solidarities, and privatised much of life, then 'community' has a significant role in re-skilling and re-animating us to be social people, to re-value the public sphere and collective action.

What is needed then is love for something else, something other than that produced during the last 40 years. It's not about a 'going back' to something of the past, nor is it advocating the rise of large state-controlled economies. Soul-force, mediated through a dialogue

---

135 Furedi, F., *Therapy Culture: Cultivating Vulnerability in an Uncertain Age* (London & New York: Routledge, 2004); Pupavac V., "War on the couch: The emotionology of the new International security paradigm", *European Journal of Social Theory*, 7/2 (2004), 149-170.

between Gandhi and Tagore, is a necessity right now in an ethical, embodied and strategic 'fight-back' where power needs to be 'taken back,' decisions re-democratised, and life re-socialised and re-beautified. And foregrounding Tagore, soul-activism needs to be more oriented towards the aesthetic: engaging with the field of desire, re-shaping cultural narratives and worldviews.

Community provides part of the solution. But to infuse community with soul, the approaches of Gandhi and Tagore need to be refined and re-interpreted in three ways. We can summarise them under three headings: internal practice, disciplined learning, and community structures.

Internal practice and core values — an ethical compass

I've mentioned truth and love as being central to Gandhi's and Tagore's personal and political thinking. Neither are terms that are easy to imagine in the context of political life; they are far away from our everyday experience of politics. It's disturbing to witness public conversations turning, in the blink of an eye, to considerations about which non-core promises can be broken. Truth is an anathema to modern politics. Love is also a far cry from the bullying, wedging and controlling that characterises political activity. Yet, from a soul perspective, truth and love can and should be the foundations of an ethical practice.

A soul perspective invites people to collectively reflect on their deep values, and consider what those values mean when translated into collective social action. Of course, soul recognises that many 'values' lie in the shadowy realm of our sub- or unconscious lives, not easily identified, and if identified, not easily welcomed. Such reflection requires the courage to turn away from the shallow world that emerges from constant chatter, distraction, and speedy decisions.

A deeper kind of reflection invites people to engage in dialogue about what values make up the good life – both privately and publicly – what myths lend depth to those values, and what political, social and cultural projects can be animated to support those values. It also requires recognition that the good life is not the same as a sanitised life. Truth and love were Gandhi's core values. What are ours?

As we have seen, these conversations are oriented towards ethics, as opposed to morality. Within this frame, morality refers to a code given from outside, while ethics refers to clarity about how we choose or struggle to live within the context of our limited freedom, infused with a vitality that keeps seeking – what Caputo calls a 'passion of not knowing.'[136] Gandhi was very clear that for him 'going with the flow' meant being a machine, to live as society wants you to live. In this sense most societies, despite their claims to offer freedom, are actually offering a very limited code to live by. In our modern times the code is rugged individualism, consumerism, competition, materialism and ... you can name the rest!

Instead, Gandhi wanted people to live another option, as ethical beings. It should be said that it's not easy to be clear about values or ethical choices; most of us need to be engaged in conversations, vigorous debate and deep reflection, even to gain a modicum of clarity. It can also be said that we usually have no idea of our own values until we come up against other, different values. Often people tend to think of their values and ethical choices as 'just normal' – the way things are done; and it's only when people travel, or find themselves surrounded by people from another ethnic culture, or sub-culture, that they 'see' their own values for what they are.

---

136 Caputo, J. D., *Deconstruction in a Nutshell: A Conversation with Jacques Derrida* (New York, USA: Fordham University Press, 1997a)

Also, people often state a value as something of an ethical stance; for example, to say 'I value egalitarianism' is to assert an ethic of minimising economic differences. However, it's only when people have the means to escape such an espoused ethic, that one can tell whether it is an ethic (a statement of value), or just a statement of interest. It is easy to state egalitarianism as an important value when you feel relatively poor, or live on a low income. However, after several years with an accumulation of wealth and possibly substantial numbers of property investments, it becomes much harder to maintain the value of egalitarianism. It was more likely to be a statement of interests, and as class position has shifted, so has the interest. Egalitarianism was seen to not be a value, but a short-lived interest. This can be true in many domains of life. As a second example, consider the value of being non-racist. All well and good; but then what occurs when you are robbed three times by someone of a particular colour (white, black, brown...)? Suddenly the reflex is "those bloody people of colour!" Racism becomes manifest.

The key point is that values are difficult to identify in the first place, are only tested in the 'fire of practice' and are particularly tested when opportunity comes to not live up to those espoused values. Maybe deep values only emerge from the crucible of these testings as they are supported by the kind of disciplined learning and community structures discussed below.

But at a deeper level, and dipping our toes into the water of the shadowy realm, sometimes our stated values are also unable to stand up to the onslaught of soul energies, often emerging from the deeper unconscious. These energies sometimes force action or choices that appear immoral or unethical from the glazed window of a world of clearly articulated ethics; yet they can only be honoured, or even without honouring tend to carry a force that simply undoes stated values anyway. They disrupt, arising from the unknown depths of our unconscious – and we often have no choice but to work with them. I'd suggest that Gandhi's reflection that 'violence is better than nothing' is recognition that he acknowledged this shadowy realm. He certainly preferred and advocated nonviolence; however, aware of the latent energies submerged within human beings, he was willing to work with violence as a force for change.

Gandhi's notion of morality, similar to my articulation of ethics, was not about deciding on a general principle – in fact he was quite against a uniformity of duty, and suspicious of formal or mechanical notions of consistency (of principle).[137] He was aware of the complexity of ethical choices, and deeply aware of the multitude of forces shaping our lives. And he was even aware of the need for compromise. What was clear is that people need to put full effort into working out their ethical compass in the midst of complex social situations.[138] Gandhi referred to this full effort as making a vow, a concept not quite palatable in our modern times. Maybe it's worth re-visiting: a soulful approach to community work, infused with soul-force, requires a vow to do our best in the situation at hand, making disciplined efforts to keep struggling for our freedom, understanding our deeper values and ethical compass, and becoming conscious of the inner unconscious shadowy realm. We can then find a 'deep inner voice' to guide us, though we should be aware of how our context can shape the way we hear such a voice.

Disciplined learning

For community workers to be steeped in soul-force, there needs to be attention to disciplined learning. After all, as already mentioned,

137 Iyer, R., *The Moral and Political Thought of Mahatma Gandhi* (Oxford: Oxford University Press, 2000), 65.
138 Ibid., 66.

the neoliberal project has been going for 40 years. Each of us has been profoundly shaped, 'trained', by that project. Our desires – for consumption, for particular freedoms, for more opportunities – have been constructed by it. So we need to consider how to re-learn, 're-train', to re-habituate ourselves.

A great deal has been written about community workers and learning,[139] but I'd like to focus here on a couple of key ideas, and include an autobiographical perspective.

Gandhi understood that for people to engage in social justice and social change work, they need to be very disciplined in their practice. Within the Gandhian tradition, people needed to learn how to: listen to the quiet inner voice that called for concerted action; be tenacious in an on-going practical, experimental search for truth; practise non-violence, from the heart as well as in strategic political action; live simply; and cultivate self-rule. Tagore added other layers, with his orientation more to honouring life than to purifying it. He wanted people to learn in a more holistic way of being, experienced through dance, song, music, and poetry, linking the analytical and the holistic modes of thinking and living together.

Drawing on the Italian revolutionary Antonio Gramsci, I like to imagine community workers learning about soul-force as the 'organic intellectuals and story-tellers' of community life.[140] They are people who dare to think and act differently in the face of the hegemony that determines how much of current social life is perceived and lived. I love the term 'organic intellectuals' because it signifies transformational intentions – that is, intentions towards transforming not only

139 For example, Westoby, P. & Shevellar, L., eds. *Learning and Mobilising for Community Development: A Radical Tradition of Community-Based Education and Training* (Surrey, UK: Ashgate Press, 2012).

140 Mayo, P., *Gramsci, Freire and Adult Education: Possibilities for Transformative Action* (London: Zed Books, 1999); Ledwith, M., *Community Development: a Critical Approach* (Bristol: Policy Press, 2005).

people's capacities to *survive* the current system, but also to *change* the actual system itself, or step outside it to create a *different* system. But I add story-tellers because I'm convinced that change will need to occur at the level of imagination, stirred up by myth — and this is the domain of story-telling.

Community workers informed by a soul perspective need the supportive spaces of transformational learning, enabling them to keep dreaming and also to hone their skills and strategies. These community workers model a new social attitude, a new caring, and a new social vision. They are people who can bring a fresh energy, and who can facilitate the awakening of awareness, imagination and powerful action. They are people who can create a fresh dialogue and hold it open with integrity, hospitality, depth, respect and solidarity. Some of the most exciting work has happened when a cadre of such community workers has come together with the intention of defending a locality, transforming a sociality, or prosecuting a cause. There is great camaraderie in the shared work. There is great resource in the soulful stories and hard-earned life experiences of any group of diverse and committed people.

Transformational learning: some personal reflections

I first learned about community work through a three-week live-in learning course in my neighbourhood in 1987. Sometimes this is known as *in situ* learning, where learning takes place in the actual space and location of the 'work.' It should include times of reflection (drawing back from action and inserting new theory or ideas, usually through reading or input from someone) and of action (getting involved in community work). This dialogical process of reflection and action is known as *praxis*, a cycle of thinking, imagining, doing, reading, listening, and conversing. Those intensive three weeks, where we did community work during mornings and evenings and reflected during the afternoons, extended into seven years of *in situ* learning that involved living in an intentional community house while being part of an intentional community network of households. People worked part-time, to earn a living, but used their free time to involve themselves in community work. There were also structured times for reflection and learning: reading groups, study circles, community organised non-accredited courses and individual mentoring sessions. The main point is that I learned on the job. It was an experiment in modernising Gandhi's ashrams for urban Australia. It still continues.

Another learning experience I have loved are my visits to Towerland in South Africa. This is a space set in the wilderness of the Langeberg Mountains of the Southern Cape. Unlike the *in situ* learning of my Brisbane neighbourhood, this learning space is focused on observation, careful attention, and reconnecting with nature and particularly the wild. The buildings are made from nature, in mud and earth, with living roofs; the workshop space is made from rock mined from the property, hand-crafted by an artisan of exceptional skill. There is no electricity other than one solar panel to charge computers. The place is mostly off the mobile network. As the sun goes down, there is a daily ritual of lighting candles, and people sit around the fire conversing about the day's journey. Everyone is subject to nature, enjoying or enduring walks from the kitchen and work space to where people sleep or do their ablutions. You cannot get away from nature, nor hide from it. Being there for a week, immersed within the wild, while studying nature, draws people into a more participatory experience. Nature is experienced *in situ*, not mediated via windows, cars, covered corridors, or electric lights. It's transformative learning, not intellectual.

Community structures

For Gandhi and Tagore, strong social movements supporting workers committed to soul-force (truth and action) also need community
structures. Towerland is one, as is the intentional community network
I mentioned above. We cannot work alone, and neither can we rely
on spontaneous community or occasional learning experiences. After
all, in the absence of such structures we are inevitably being educated by the current economically-oriented systems that structure our
lives. This current education drives us and skills us to be individually
oriented, to work for ourselves, to save for ourselves, and to carry
the burden of our future alone (through insurance, purchasing more
property investments, or accumulating a large superannuation fund).
In summary, we are being educated by current structures of economic
policies and practices to be non-social beings. That's not to say that
each person cannot find ways of retaining social orientations, but the
educating and structuring orients in another direction.

What Gandhi and Tagore recognised is that radical learning should
reorient us towards the social — to community, and to intentional
moral, political and labouring ideals, including for Tagore the aesthetic. We need to experience community, all the more since we are committed to working with people, and rediscover its beauty along with its
challenges and dangers. The seeking of truth, nonviolence, self-rule,
and related values and ideals, are learned not in the classroom nor
from a textbook, but in the context of community life.

So alongside learning, we also need community structures that
provide regular rhythms to the work of community action and reflection. Such structures ensure the regular gathering of community workers for reflection. They promote reflective practice, and they
introduce a rhythm of dialogue that keeps us sharp in our thought,
expansive in our quest for truth, and thirsty for depth.

At the heart of Gandhi's community structures were *ashrams,* places that were homes as well as learning spaces for community activists. Crucial to these structures was the integration of the personal and the political, most clearly demonstrated by the involvement of all ashram members in domestic duties, food growing, cleaning toilets and all the daily tasks of maintenance. The ashram way of life mirrored at a practical level, the way of life advocated politically. For example, reflecting on our own lives, how often do we find ourselves arguing for inclusive policies but failing to live inclusive lives? Are we for hospitality towards asylum-seekers in the policy sphere, but unable to include asylum-seekers around our table for dinner?

For Tagore the key community structures were both his school called Santiniketan, which started as an ashram but was also a place where he was deeply committed to the creation of a new kind of world university that could 'hold' both the social and the spiritual; and his Institute for Rural Reconstruction, later named Shriniketan or 'Abode of Welfare', focused on agronomy and social experimentation.[141] His pedagogical inclinations were towards the aesthetic, with students learning dance, art, poetry, languages, and literature, as well as agricultural labour and social literacy.

In contemporary times, and particularly within Australia, ashrams are not the norm, and neither are world universities such as those experimented with by Tagore. Although there has been a rich history of intentional communities, the main forms of community structure take on local flavours – as CBOs, NGOs, foundations, co-operatives, and networks. These community structures can then become the places and spaces where people are potentially re-socialised, where they learn to

---

141 Shriniketan was started by Tagore along with economist and agronomist Leonard Knight Elmhirst, who also later on, along with his wife, founded Dartington Hall, in Devon, UK – see also Postscript below.

'rub up against' others, those who have different views. It is where they experience the beauty of belonging and participation alongside the difficulties that occur when people try to live and work together.

Soul-force as a crisis response

The human species would appear to be at a crossroads, a juncture, a crisis point. Anyone who denies this is simply living with his or her head in the sand. The soul of the world invites awareness of the earth's suffering, and in turn awareness of our own suffering. We are deeply alienated from the earth, and also it could be argued from one another and even ourselves.

A response to this crisis is soul-force: collective social action and social disobedience that flows from a considered reflection on the particular political-economic, social and especially cultural forces at work in the world. Beautiful resistances are required, and I've suggested that this requirement can be supported by reflective spaces to consider our deeper values, by disciplined learning, and also through community structures that provide platforms for regular reflection and action. Building social movements needs these ingredients, and soul infuses this building with attention of practice, to the shadow realms, the mythological, the energies at play. Let's dance between Gandhi and Tagore, learning from their inspirational lives and writings, all the while listening deeply to our own vocational callings.

<u>POEM</u>

<u>TRANSLATED FROM A</u>

<u>WORDLESS LANGUAGE</u>

Homes are quietly burning:
Madness on the march.
Lies move unresisted
Through the land

We stand by helpless
As our lives are occupied
Faster than we
understand.

Collaborators wave
their little flags
As ugliness takes over;
"MAKE A FRIEND OF
UGLINESS" they say,
"LEARN THE LANGUAGE.
THEN YOU WON'T GET HURT"

But you will —
No matter how
you crawl;
A knock on the door
one night,
A scuffle in the hall
Your heart rubbed
in the dirt

"Alright!" You scream your
indecision,
"Take the children — but
leave the television!"
So you stand by useless
As childhood is trashed;
Innocence reviled;
The truth is bashed

The home and the
idea of home
Is set on fire.
And still you stand by
As the goodness in your
culture burns
You stand there in
the glow.
Going, going —
Going with the flow.

Ah yes, THE FLOW!
Heaven help us.
ONE DAY you might
Be asked, "how come
You did not know
What was going on?
Why did you not fight?"

"FIGHT?" you'll say
"that's a thought that
never occurred."
The very word
brings tears."
It will dawn on
you after all those
painful years
That to fight is one
of the most beautiful,
simple and useful ideas.

Leunig

Conclusion

I N HIS most recent work *The Bush*, Don Watson depicts a particular kind of 'old' rural life:

> To be a farmer, first let the iron into your soul; if dejection should also get in before you close the gate it, too, is part of your lot. It is not practical to mourn the death of a wombat or bandicoot: one may as well mourn the pig that owes its existence to your liking for bacon. A good dog one may mourn a little, because a good dog is a loyal servant to men and women and seems to understand their needs, but one should never make a fuss about these things.[142]

He then goes on in the next page to say,

> In the daily contest with nature the women were as determined as the men, as faithful to the cause. But the women made exceptions to the surviving birds. They talked to them, treated them in the garden as companions and friends; saw in them, possibly, the intimations of grace ...[143]

---

142 Watson, D., *The Bush: Travels in the heart of Australia* (Melbourne, Australia: Hamish Hamilton, an imprint of Penguin Books, 2014), 5.
143 Ibid., 6.

Watson has expressed something here that is relevant to what we have been discussing. Maybe his reflections seem far away; most of the readers of this book will be urban dwellers, or at least suburban fringe dwellers. There will be few or no memories of or relations with the old-timers working hard in the bush on the frontier. For many of us, at least for Australians, we have instead a life of privilege in one of the wealthiest countries on the planet. We can have almost anything we want, and go most anywhere, anytime. And yet Watson seems to pinpoint something, about a kind of masculinity in particular, that is averse to sinking into the experience of grief and loss, the reality that is before him. The farmer gets on with things – he does his daily work. Mourning is for weaklings. Fair enough too, on the frontier.

But for the rest of us, the majority of us not on the frontier, maybe there's a different way to be. We should avoid letting the 'iron into our soul.' There's a clear invitation here: let's mourn the loss of our dogs, and much more. And Watson's playful image of the women talking to the birds as companions is one that provides food for the soul. Here's an image of hope on the borderlands, making the garden alive and being made alive by the intimacy that emerges through talking to the animals. Martin Buber discovered this potential through an encounter with a horse. A world of dialogue unfolded for him. Martin Shaw was awakened to the world, and therefore to himself, through four years of living in a tent on the wild hills of Dartmoor. We need to enter the borderlands, the in-between spaces between the inner and outer, the familiar and unfamiliar, the village and the forest, the frontier and the city. Dwelling in the silent, shadowy realms, soul has more chance of emerging.

The point is that, working against soul – with 'iron in the soul,' in those Watsonesque images of the frontier – it's terrifying to sink into the experience, the simple being of what is unfolding. Many clamour for control instead. I hope to push community workers in the other direction, towards a sinking into soul, without too much iron, comfortable with not being in control.[144] It's soul-work that is able to respond to the elemental in life – fire, earth, water and air. We need fire to get out and do the hard farm work, or its social equivalent of community 'leg-work'. Earthwork demands that we remain grounded in the *realpolitik* of strategy, projects, measuring, being accountable, and seeking funds. The work of air is to dream the airy vision of what might be; while our 'water work' requires us to respond carefully, with agility, in the dance that makes community work practice alive to possibilities and potential in the living social situation. It's about not resisting what's unfolding within and without, in the world and in a social situation. It's about sinking into the social situation, discerning the energies at play, the latent, the subtle, even the sacred.

Community workers pretty well always work with people. That's a given. And people are curious creatures, alive to mysterious ways of being and doing things. There is also a deep plurality at play within 'community', because when all these mysterious people get together, holding their difference, then there is a powerful dialogue within people, between people and of making 'the group'. The mysteries of their individual lives are multiplied exponentially when a group works together. The individuals and the group co-exist and co-create what emerges. Basically a group is a *huge* mystery. As already mentioned in the Introduction, I use the term mystery in the sense that things seem mysterious unless we 'see with new eyes'. The mystery is an illusion: we just have become insensitive to seeing the invisible. So I've drawn on this language of soul as a way of trying to see some of these invisible energies and mysteries at work.

144 Of course, as mythologist Robert Bly reminds us, warriors do need some iron! See Bly, *Iron John,* 178.

Community workers are also shaped by the myths and energies they bring to the work. We've talked about the inability of a community worker to control any community work process. The challenge is to fully be in the process, both in the group alive to its energies, and alive to the individuals, while also standing outside the group, trying to observe what is occurring, and feeding back that observation to the group, triggering a dialogue and potentially a growing consciousness. This is the work of transformation, the living and genuine work of building community within the official processes. It's the work of responsive dancing, *vacilando*! These ideas, these movements represent something of what I am imaging or imagining as a soulful approach to community work.

The real knack, and here I'm thinking about soulful professional wisdom, is to enter all community work situations alive to the particularity of the story unfolding. There's something dangerous about familiarity with community processes. Familiarity leads to contempt, to deadness, blandness, to categorisation, abstraction, to distancing. Yet to come to each community work situation, alive to the mysteries at play, alive to the vibrant, authentic stories emerging – within each individual and the emerging group, to the forces and fields at work shaping the group, the practitioner and the context – enables the practitioner to see with new eyes.

We will also become aware of our blindness, because at the end of the day we rarely see accurately. Such seeing and awareness of blindness can only cultivate a passion for knowing, a passion for the other, a passion for 'the work' of community work. When we think we know something, we're often dead to it; the journey of curious and passionate searching ends. So this questing and questioning passion, this participatory and anticipatory presence to the social situation, sits at the heart of being alive, not dead. When alive the process will

feel animated and authentic. It will feed the soul whilst also challenging and disrupting easy pathways. This aliveness does not avoid suffering — suffering of self, of others and the world. To be alive means
to be vulnerable to the suffering of the world, the soul of the world,
which might mean 'falling down', feeling weak. But it comes from a
sense of not being distant and dead, but of being alive.

Within these four core chapters, I've played with the ideas of soul,
soulful, soul of the world and soul-force. Each chapter provides a
glimpse into the possibilities of how this living, embodied, animated
idea of soul can be imagined in relation to community work. Within
Chapter One, soul itself was explored through the eyes of several authors and I tried to provide some signposts of how soul might relate
to community work. In Chapter Two, soulful was explored in relation to awareness of self in community work practice and the 'practice' itself. Soul shines a light on the ways in which transformational
community work often develops within the official work, and how a
community worker informed by a soul perspective can attend to what
is occurring within a social situation. I gave particular attention to a
soulful form of professional wisdom.

Chapter Three's musings on soul of the world, closely linked to
James Hillman and Mary Watkins' work, started to shape a framework of practice that foregrounds an understanding of soul beyond
an individual frame. The soul of the world invites a deeper engagement with the current suffering of the planet and the evidence of an
accompanying social and spiritual suffering. Alienation undoes us,
disconnecting us from self, others, and the planet. A re-weaving of
connection is required for deep healing, and yet it seems that this can
only occur as people become aware that, to quote Yeats, "things fall
apart". Manic living helps people avoid such awareness, but assuming
that avoidance is not possible forever, and that some consciously turn

away from it, then the soul of the world can be heard, and change can be invited. Soul-force, the focus of Chapter Four, can then be the rich resource that sustains social change using collective approaches. Tapping into deep values, and shadow energies, can help sustain our collective efforts. Disciplined learning is no doubt needed, along with community structures than enable us to sustain action and reflection in the work. Together, such values, learning and structures can 'hold', or provide a container for our ongoing work for social change and social justice.

In all these processes, soul helps us know when to do inner work, and also when to take to marching. We can become attentive to the nudge of the soul, the movements that lead to either of these places – the forest or the village, the ashram or the streets. Soul undertakes to at times be asleep and then be awake, to disrupt what our ego might assume to be right. I might feel it's time to go into a meditation retreat, this desire might represent a movement of soul, and yet soul could also burst forth disrupting this idea and demand social action. Meaning is made only as something occurs, or in hindsight. At the moment of disruption it's often just plain bloody difficult. It's a case of surrendering and moving with the energies at play in the self, in a group and the world. It's a ride, an adventure, and a journey. It's tough, rough and mad. It's alive, animated and full!

I have often mused over Latin American commentator Oscar Guardiola-Rivera's idea that we live in an era of a war of paradigms – between an industrial and indigenous paradigm of development.[145] Within this framing of the challenge, the industrial paradigm represents an unfettered expansion of modernity, 'globalisation from

145 Guardiola-Rivera. O., *What if Latin America Ruled the World? How the South Will Take the North Through the 21st Century* (London, Berlin, New York: Bloomsbury, 2010).

above' and rampant surplus accumulation. Community work can then become a tool of modernity's impulse and trajectory. Alternatively, when community work is guided by an indigenous or decolonising paradigm, it can potentially contribute to reconnection to nature/ mother earth, revitalisation of the commons, and more radical and robust practices of resistance to some aspects of modernity.

A soulful perspective on community work could enter into a creative dialogue with indigenous visions. Indigenous cosmology gets soul – it's open to the subtle and sacred. It has a long, even an eternal time dimension, aware that the deeper things of life and community work take time. It's aware of the gentle nudges of the soul; an example within First Nations people of Australia would be 'going walk-about', alluding to the importance of the soul knowing how to hold the inner and the outer, the work of community and the work of connecting self to source, via a sojourn in wild nature. Indigenous cosmology is also attentive to the soul of the world, understanding the reciprocal, participatory, anticipatory nature of human-earth relations. The inner work, or interiority as I have called it, requires not only a turning inwards, but a contextual sense awakening engagement with wild nature. Otherwise interiority can easily become introspection and disengagement. Caring for country is to care for soul, and vice versa.

Within indigenous cosmology there is also an astute awareness of soul as field of influence, with a consciousness that rampant desire of objects, things, items, which are in turn rendered dead by a dualistic world-view, undoes the self and community, directing energy towards material and technological acquisition. This acquisitiveness creates zombies and cyborgs, living a falsely harmonious life within 'Team Australia'. It's deadly, and death becoming us. It's certainly the opposite of vitalism, fuelled by an ethical impulse towards freedom, love, plurality, careful conflicting and robust conversation.

So let's learn from indigenous life, from our First Nations people. Michael Leunig gets the idea; it's partly why his work adds visual and humorous texture to this written text. Let's get down on our knees, let's talk to the duck, let's find people who also live with ducks, and also those who don't; those who sing to birds and even those with iron in their souls, and let's do soulful community work together!

I'd like to conclude with the idea that we live in an historical moment, calling for particularly powerful energies. These energies include all those of the lover, the warrior, the king, the magician, and dare I say the trickster. I've personally been in the grasp of trickster energy for some months now — the energies that flow in the realm of borderlands, forcing a crossing over from one life to another, disrupting, destroying even. I think we're at a time in history where trickster energy is at work, crossing from industrial visions, versions and dogmas of development to something 'other', something new. It's scary stuff as old certainties fall apart to be opened to the new. I'm wondering what might be community work's contribution to this 'new', as we open ourselves to trickster energy. It's not a new set of dogmas about how to be in the world, but as I have implied, it is to enact a particular set of practices with one another, in co-operation with each other, but in the spirit of total openness to the unfolding journey, letting go of control.

Of course it's not only about trickster energy. By god we need plenty of lover energy too, animating us to care and be passionate towards one another. We desperately need mature kingly energy, able to make wise decisions. Community work's kingly moments are astute analysis, the narrative thread that forges a way forward within the multiplicity of thoughts and ideas that a group of people will inevitably create. Magician energy would also be helpful, enabling us to consider the broader perspective, to understand the whole, and see into the cracks where the light might come in. And finally, we need warrior energy, maybe more than ever, energising us with soul-force willing to fight for change, and confronting the forces standing against change.

Postscript: Soulful threads

Michael Leunig has been a long-lasting prophet of the soul. He's been a companion on the journey since, well, I can't remember — it seems like forever. Hence the inclusion of his cartoons. But I can remember other soul companions, when I met them and how they have supported me in my community work journey. Their companionship provides threads of a life that attempts to understand soul and social change in balance. Here are some of those threads.

I was introduced to Thomas Moore's *Care of the Soul*[146] in 1995 after experiencing a love crisis, having just migrated to South Africa for several years of work. James Hillman's *The Soul's Code*[147] cut deep into my worldview the same year, at a similar time to meeting Verne Harris, who became an ever-present soul-mate. Moore and Hillman demand, insist, along with Verne, on regular revisits to their vital imagination. Copies of their books sit on that bookshelf which is re-

146 Moore, *Care of the Soul: How to Add Depth and Meaning to Your Everyday Life*.
147 Hillman, J., *The Soul's Code* (New York: Random House, 1996).

served for 'never throwing away, never to be left behind'. Their work helps me attend to the complexities of the inner life with a subtle, nuanced, mythic attention to rhythm and timing. Maybe rhythm and timing are the keys to a good life.

Whilst Moore and Hillman help attend to the inner life, or more accurately, have helped me discover the inner therapist within myself, there are also those companions in the outer life of soul. I have already referred to Dave Andrews' and Anthony Kelly's introduction of Gandhi's work and practices, particularly soul-force, in the late 80s. The late 80s and early 90s were years of protest, against the first Iraq war and Australia's complicity in it, the training of Indonesian troops in Canungra, and a host of other urgent issues. The Catholic Worker community down the road, in Boundary Street, West End, inspired me as I experimented in intentional living at the Bristol Street Community. They were heady days of cultivating an inner life while participating in solidarity work. Soul required attention to the movements between the two. I had to learn how to build courage, and what it means to not react violently when Queensland police are twisting your ears in an attempt to break a blockade.

My understanding of Gandhi deepened through living in South Africa, the place that radicalised him, shifting his vocation from a lawyer to a leader of civil disobedience. His twenty years of work there, often forgotten, forged a culture that understood the role of nonviolent social action which we know carried forward to a negotiated transition to black majority rule in 1994: Tutu, Mandela, Biko, Slovo, Thambo, Hani – all towers of strength themselves, but indebted to Gandhi. In 2007, about to take up a position as a lecturer in community development at The University of Queensland, I knew that it was time to revisit the life of Gandhi, and so I set off on a three-month pilgrimage to India, to visit his grave, to listen to the people of

India. I travelled there with a dusty and broken copy of Paulo Freire's *Pedagogy of the Oppressed*[148] and realised I had a lot to learn about dialogue and social change. Freire had profoundly influenced Steve Biko in South Africa in the 1970s, such that Biko's Black Community Programmes were modelled on some of Freire's work.[149] That Indian journey was catalysed in the *opus* of Freire's work while feasting on that other experimenter in a life of dialogue, Martin Buber.

In 1993 as part of my postgraduate education with Anthony Kelly I studied E.F. Schumacher's *Small is Beautiful*[150]: one author-activist chosen from a substantial list. Schumacher's Buddhist economics and 'small is beautiful' vision for the world has stuck with me ever since, inspiring a life of trying to live simply, socially and in solidarity with those on the margins (and those aspects of myself easily marginalised too). The circle turned when, after many years of dreaming, I spent some time at Schumacher College in October 2013. Here was a learning space, a place of innovation combining the economic and ecological vision of Schumacher, the poetic-aesthetic soul of Tagore, under the leadership of the ever-inspiring pilgrim of peace Satish Kumar. Kumar's work had influenced me for many years, challenging me to live a life of the pilgrim while being engaged socially. The title of his most recent work *Soil, Soul and Society*,[151] depicting his Trinitarian vision for modern life, says it all. I love the brief insights into his own biography with pearls of wisdom such as this:

> From the age of 9 to 18 I was not only taught to practise non-violence to all living beings and to practise self-restraint but also to

148 Freire, *Pedagogy of the Oppressed*.
149 See my account of this influence in Westoby, *Theorising The Practice of Community Development – a South African Perspective*.
150 Schumacher, *Small is Beautiful*.
151 Kumar, S., *Soil, Soul and Society: a new trinity for our time* (East Essex, UK: Leaping Hare Press, 2013).

develop soul qualities by long and deep meditation, by the practice of day-long silence once a week, by fasting for one day a month and by standing in solitude and stillness in the wild.[152]

To experience deep connection and holism between earth, self and others is the life challenge, and this kind of experiencing represents what Joanna Macy has astutely referred to as the Great Turning. It's worth hoping, and watering the seeds of that hope.

Schumacher College in Devon also sits within the grounds of Dartington Hall, and over Easter they usually celebrate the Tagore Festival there. They have managed to understand the deep connection between soul and social change, between the inner and outer, the aesthetic and politic. Tagore continues to inspire these connections and his influence continues to regularly amaze me.

In 2011 I was invited to speak at a community work educator conference in Dublin. I can still vividly remember stepping outside of my hotel and crossing the road to stroll in St. Stephen's Green. Somewhat jetlagged and in that fuzzy state where the soul hasn't yet caught up with the body, in the corner of my eye I caught a glimpse of a beautifully-sculptured bust. I was drawn to it and realised it was of Tagore, friend of the great Irish poet Yeats. Yeats wrote the preface to *Gitanjali*, the poem that won Tagore the Nobel Prize in Literature, and here was Ireland paying homage to Tagore – a land that somehow understands how to hold together a terrible history of loss, the defiance of political action, along with soul: maintaining the music, so to speak, along with a good taste for a pint of Guinness.

Weaving such connections, finding a story of how soul keeps calling in my own life, awakens the mythic element to life. We can cast aside the serendipitous moments, or the awakening of chance

---

152 Ibid., 64.

encounters, or the arrival in a place deeply sought for many years. Or we can choose to meditate on the meaning that can be made from these experiences. Soul keeps calling me to make meaning. These author-activists, the many soul-companions keep calling, keep inviting, keep insisting: "Maintain the passion of searching. Don't give up, don't give in, but arise to the moment that is upon us, demanding something new of each of us, of our community work practice, of our social change dreaming."

We must make do with scraps.....

Little scraps of
peace and quiet.
Hope, conversation, handshakes,
– all in dribs and drabs.

A few crumbs of fun
A tiny flake of beauty.
One teaspoon of enthusiasm.

Off-cuts of each other
A skerrick of
   community…
A bit of a kiss.

A snippet of eye contact.
A snippet of hospitality.
A snippet of patience.

A shred of honor.
A wisp of good humor.
A sample of compassion.

Leftovers, oddments,
remnants of the glorious
situation.
A fragment of God.
Not much really.
Sorry. Time's up.

Leunig

Example Workshop: Community Work with Soul

This example is based on a workshop I have previously facilitated with Howard Buckley of Community Praxis Co-operative (www.communitypraxis.org).

The current program was designed for a full one-day workshop. Many activities could easily be given more time, and the process extended to one-and-a-half to two days.

Objectives of the workshop are to:

- Explore some dimensions of community work within the realm of soul, such as depth and enchantment – asking questions related to what captivates us in our hopes and imaginings for a better world
- Foreground our skills in attention, observation and developing 'an interpretation,' enabling a responsive dance with the world around us
- Deepen our commitment to a powerful soul-force.

Resources needed:

- Cardboard, pens, scissors and pins for name tags
- A3 cardboard for people to draw their framework
- Box of pens, and a pile of crayons for drawing.

Handouts:

- Story of practice from Chapter One of this book
- 10 cartoons from this book
- Chapter Four of this book
- Evaluation form.

Methodology of workshop

The workshop will utilise the spiral method as the guiding frame. Within stage 3 (Insert new information and theory) different 'texts' and stories related to soul will be drawn upon. Below is the spiral model depicted pictorially.

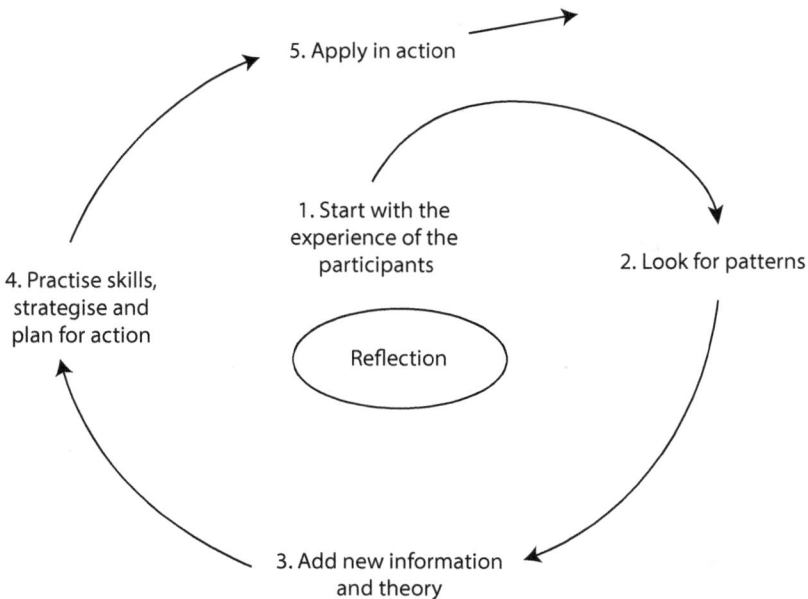

Introduction
Setting the scene

- Let participants know that we'd prefer to avoid intellectual debates about the concept or meaning of soul. The goal of the workshop is not to define soul.
- Take some time to work out with the participants the 'ground rules' for the workshop, such that everyone feels safe to participate.
- Explain the process via spiral approach (see image above).
- Take some time for everyone to introduce himself or herself.

Session #1
Start with people's experiences

Invite people individually, to respond to or continue the following sentences:

- I have come to a workshop on community work with soul because...
- I feel most grounded and in my body when...
- I feel vitality in my practice when I am doing...
- In my heart of heart I yearn to...
- I feel most exhausted when I...

In pairs share those sentences; maybe elicit from the other person what could be shared with the larger group ... get to know each other in more depth.

In plenary people share what they would like to share about themselves from those sentences.

Session #2
Look for patterns

- The two facilitators can share with everyone what they 'heard' from the group within plenary;
- Others can add to this as they wish;
- One possibility is to also draw on a large sheet of paper in the centre of the circle a depiction of patterns or ideas emerging from the discussion.

Morning Tea

Session #3
Adding new information and theory (drawing on Freirean triggers/ codes to elicit discussion). There are several options for this. If there is time both can be incorporated into the workshop. Each is presented below.

Option 1: A case study exploration of what is soulful community work.

Resource: Use story from Chapter One of the book.

- Main objective: To talk through official and orthodox kinds of community work
- Secondary objective: To elicit some initial thoughts about community work with soul.

- *Step 1: Read or tell the story*
- *Step 2: Ask:* What can you identify as orthodox or official community work processes?
- *Step 3: Ask:* What might we see as spirited elements within this story? (Vision/aspiration/goals)

- *Step 4: Ask:* What might illustrate soulful elements of community work practice or processes?
- *Step 5: Ask:* Does anyone have a story they'd like to tell that illustrates other elements?

Option 2: A group discussion after watching the video clip on soulful community work.

- *Step 1:* Everyone watches the video clip 'Community Work as Soul', https://www.youtube.com/watch?v=-bfAqKprHco
- *Step 2:* In groups of three, discuss some thoughts that arose from the 'lecture'
- *Step 3:* In plenary, discuss larger issues about soul, soulful, soul of the world and soul-force.

Lunch

Session #4
Warm-up after lunch: Do anything with your body that reflects how you feel right now! - one person at a time so that everyone else can see (and laugh)

Exercise #1
- Invite people to enjoy the Leunig cartoons in this book, or chosen from Leunig's archive. Ask people to pick one cartoon that resonates with how they are starting to imagine community work with soul looks like. Ask people to be prepared to come and share the story of their experience of the cartoon and the reason chosen.

Exercise #2

- This is an imaginative exercise on courage and our work, and is linked to the material in Chapter Four of the book.
- Remember a time in in your life or community work practice when you felt really fearful – what did it feel like, how did your body respond, what did your mind do? Now remember a time when you had to draw on courage in your life or community work practice? What did that feel like; how did your body respond; what did your mind do? What happened?
- Debrief – how did it feel?
- What does this mean for community work that incorporates soul-force?

Afternoon Tea

Reflection as a group

This session involves participants spending some time alone drawing a 'framework' of community work with soul, gathering the wisdom elicited from the previous sessions. It involves organising the 'data' so to speak from the discussions and putting it together in a picture/symbol form. There are several configurations of the picture that can be used (linear steps, circle with each dimension equal, or soul at centre and dimensions emerging from that centre, and so forth).

Consideration of application in action

Ask people to (i) share their frameworks, and (ii) meaning for shifts in practice as people return to their workplace/vocation.

Evaluation and closure

References

Aizenstat, S. 2012. 'Fragility of the World's Dream', in Merlini, F. Sullivan, L. Bernardini, R. & Olson, K. (eds). *Eranon Yearbook 2009-2011: Love on a Fragile Thread,* Daimon Verlag

Bauman, Z. & Bordoni, C. 2014. *State of Crisis,* Cambridge: Polity Press

Beradi, Franco, "Bifo". 2009. *The Soul at Work: From Alienation to Autonomy,* LA, California: Semiotext (e).

Bly, R. 1990. *Iron John,* Dorset: Element Books Limited.

Buber, M., 1947. *Between Man and Man. London and New York*: Routledge & Kegan Paul.

Caputo, J. D. (ed.) 1997a. *Deconstruction in a Nutshell: A Conversation with Jacques Derrida,* New York: Fordham University Press.

Caputo, J. D. 1997. *The Prayers and Tears of Jacques Derrida: Religion Without Religion,* Bloomington & Indianapolis: Indiana University Press.

Carey, G. 2014. *Moving Among Strangers,* The University of Queensland Press, QLD, Australia.

Connolly, W. 2013. *The Fragility of Things: Self-Organising, Processes, Neoliberal Fantasies, and Democratic Activism,* Durham & London: Duke University Press.

Derrida, J. 2001. *On Cosmopolitanism*, New York: Routledge.

Dunne, J., 2011. "Professional Wisdom" in "Practice". In Bondi, L., Carr, D., Clark, C. and Clegg, C., eds., *Towards Professional Wisdom: Practical Deliberation in the People Professions.* Surrey, UK: Ashgate.

Esteva, G., Babones, S., & Babcicky, P., 2013 *The Future of Development: A Radical Manifesto.* Bristol, UK: Policy Press.

Freire, P., 1970/2006. *Pedagogy of the Oppressed.* New York: Continuum.

Furedi, F. 2004. *Therapy Culture: Cultivating Vulnerability in an Uncertain Age*, London & New York: Routledge.

Gardner, 2011. *Critical Spirituality: A Holistic Approach to Contemporary Practice,* Ashgate.

Gandhi, M. 1910, *Hind Swaraj.* Phoenix, Natal: The International Printing Press.

Geels, F.W. & Kemp, R., 2012, 'The multi-level perspective as a new perspective for studying socio-technical transitions', in: Geels, F.W., Kemp, R., Dudley, G. and Lyons, G. (eds.), 2012, *Automobility in Transition? A Socio-Technical Analysis of Sustainable Transport*, London: Routledge.

Gros, F. 2014. *A Philosophy of Walking,* London: Verso Books.

Guardiola-Rivera. O. 2010. *What if Latin America Ruled the World? How the South Will Take the North Through the 21st Century*, London, Berlin, New York: Bloomsbury.

Gupta, U. D. (ed) 2006. *Rabindranath Tagore: My Life In My Words*, New Delhi: Penguin Books India.

Hanh, T. N. 2009. *You Are Here: Discovering the Magic of the Present Moment,* Boston & London, Shambhala Library.

Harding, S. 2006. *Animate Earth: Science, Intuition and Gaia,* Cambridge, UK: Green Books.

Hill, B. 2014. *Peacemongers,* The University of Queensland Press: Queensland, Australia.

Hillman, J. 1977. *Re-Visioning Psychology*, New York: First Harper Colophon.

Hillman, J. 1992. *The thought of the heart and the soul of the world*, Connecticut: Spring Publications.

Hillman, J. 1996. *The Soul's Code*, New York: Random House

Hillman, J. 1983. *Interviews*, Connecticut: Spring Publications.

Hillman, J. 2006."Aesthetic Response as Political Action", in *City and Soul*, ed. R.J. Leaver: 143.

Hillman, J. 1998 *Insearch*, Connecticut: Woodstock

Hillman, J. 1964. *Suicide and the Soul*, Connecticut: Spring Publications.

Iyer, R. 2000. *The Moral and Political Thought of Mahatma Gandhi*, Oxford: Oxford University Press.

Jullien, F. 2007. *Vital Nourishment: Departing from Happiness*, New York: Zone Books.

Jullien, F. 2011. *The Silent Transformations*, London, New York, Calcutta: Seagull Books.

Kaplan, A., 2002. *Development Practitioners and Social Process: Artists of the Invisible*. Chicago and London: Pluto Press.

Kelly, Anthony, n.d., *Working with Communities*, Centre for Social Response.

Kornfield, J. 1993. *A Path With Heart*, USA & Canada: Bantam Books.

Kumar, S. 2013. *Soil, Soul and Society: a new trinity for our time*, East Essex, UK: Leaping Hare Press.

Ledwith, M. 2005. *Community Development: a Critical Approach*, Bristol: Policy Press.

Lyons, K. & Westoby, P. 2014. 'Carbon Colonialism and the New Land Grab: Plantation Forestry in Uganda and its Livelihood Impacts', in *Journal of Rural Studies*. Vol. 36. pp. 13-21.

Macy, J. and Brown, M. Y., 1998. *Coming Back to Life: Practices to Reconnect Our Lives, Our World*. Gabriola Island, BC: New Society Publishers.

Manne, A. 2014. *The Life of I: The New Culture of Narcissism,* Australia: University of Melbourne Press.

Max-Neef, M., 1991. *Human Scale Development: Conceptions, Application and Further Reflections.* London and New York: The Apex Press.

Mayo, P. 1999. *Gramsci, Freire and Adult Education: Possibilities for Transformative Action,* London: Zed Books.

Moore, T., ed. 1989. *A Blue Fire: James Hillman,* Harperperennial.

Moore, T. 1992. *Care of the Soul: How to Add Depth and Meaning to Your Everyday Life,* London: Judy Piakkus Publishers Ltd.

Moore, T. 1996. *The Re-Enchantment of Everyday Life,* Sydney: Hodder & Stoughton.

Nussbaum, M. 2010. *Not For Profit: Why Democracy Needs The Humanities,* Princeton and New York: Princeton University Press.

Palmer, P. 2000. *Let Your Life Speak: Listening for the Voice of Vocation,* San Francisco: Jossey-Bass.

Platanov, A, 1999. *Soul.* London: Vintage Books.

Plotkin, B. 2003. *Soulcraft: Crossing into the Mysteries of Nature and Psyche,* California, USA: New World Library.

Pupavac V. 2004. 'War on the couch: The emotionology of the new International security paradigm', *European Journal of Social Theory,* 7(2): 149-170.

Rose, N. 1999. *Powers of Freedom: Reframing Political Thought,* Cambridge University Press, Cambridge.

Rose, N. 1989. *Governing the Soul: The shaping of the private self,* Free Association Books, London & New York.

Salecl, R. 2010. *Choice,* Profile Books, London.

Scharmer, O. & Kaufer, K. 2013. *Leading from the Emergent Future,* Berrett-Koehler Publishers, California, USA.

Schon, D., 1983. *The Reflective Practitioner: How Professionals Think in Action.* London: Ashgate.

Schumacher, E. F., 1974. *Small is Beautiful: Economics as if People Mattered.* London: Abacus.

Sennett, R., 2012. *Together: The Rituals, Pleasures and Politics of Cooperation.* London and New York: Penguin Press Group.

Shaw, M. 2011. *A Branch in the Lightening Tree: Ecstatic Myth and the Grace in Wildness,* Ashland, Oregon: White Cloud Press.

Steinbeck, J. 1939. *The Grapes of Wrath,* USA: The Viking Press.

Steinbeck, J. 1962. *Travels with Charlie,* Folio Books, London.

Stow, R. 1963. *Tourmaline,* Australia, Macdonald and Co.

Tacey, D. 2013. *The Darkening Spirit: Jung, Spirituality,* Religion. London & NY: Routledge.

Tacey, 2000. *Re-Enchantment: The New Australian Spirituality.* Sydney: HarperCollins.

Trinca, H. & Fox, C. 2004. *Better than Sex: How a whole generation got hooked on sex,* Random House Australia, NSW, Australia.

Watkins, M. and Shulman, H. 2008a. *Toward Psychologies of Liberation,* Basingstoke and New York: Palgrave Macmillan.

Watkins, M. 2008b. 'Breaking the Vessels: Archetypal Psychology and the Restoration of Culture, Community, and Ecology', in Marlan, S. (ed). *Archetypal Psychologies: Reflections in honour of James Hillman edition,* p. 414-437. New Orleans, LA: Spring Books and Journals.

Watson, D. 2014. *The Bush: Travels in the heart of Australia,* Melbourne, Australia: Hamish Hamilton, an imprint of Penguin Books.

Westoby. P. 2014. *Theorising The Practice of Community Development – a South African Perspective,* Surrey, UK: Ashgate.

Westoby, P. and Dowling, G., 2009. *Dialogical Community Development: With Depth, Solidarity and Hospitality.* Brisbane, Australia: Tafına Press.

Westoby, P. and Dowling, G. 2013. *Theory and Practice of Dialogical Community Development: International Perspectives.* London: Routledge.

Westoby, P. & Kaplan, A. 2014. 'Foregrounding Practice – Reaching for a responsive and ecological approach to community development – A conversational inquiry into the dialogical and developmental frameworks of community development', in *Community Development Journal*. 49 (2), pp.214-227.

Westoby, P. & Lyons, K. 2015. We would rather die in jail fighting for land, than die of hunger": A Ugandan case study examining the ambiguous deployment of corporate-led corporate-led community development in the green economy *Community Development Journal* doi:10.1093/cdj/bsv005.

Westoby, P. & Shevellar, L. eds. 2012. *Learning and Mobilising for Community Development: A Radical Tradition of Community-Based Education and Training*. Surrey, UK: Ashgate Press.

Westoby, P. & Shevellar, L. 2014. 'Beware the Trojan Horse of Professionalization: A Response to de Beer et al.', in *Africanus: The South African Development Association Journal*. Vol. 44 (1) 2014 pp. 67-74.

Wheen, F. 2004. *How Mumbo-Jumbo Conquered the World*, Harper Perennial.

White, M. 1996. 'On ethics and the spiritualties of the surface', Hoyt, M. F. (eds). *Constructive Therapies*, Vol. 2.

Whyte, D. 2002. *The Heart Aroused*, London, UK: Industrial Society.

Wink, W. 1992. *Engaging the Powers: Discernment and Resistance in a World of Domination*, Minneapolis: Fortress Press.

Index

Z

About the author

Peter originally hails from the UK but now loves living in Brisbane, Australia. He is currently Senior Lecturer in Community Development at the University of Queensland, and Research Fellow at the University of the Free State, South Africa. He is also a director/consultant with Community Praxis Cooperative.

His experience includes work in Australia, the Philippines, PNG, South Africa, Vanuatu and Uganda. His interests are in forced migration studies, dialogue theory and practice, and community development.

He is passionate about running, reading, good coffee, hanging out at his local Avid Reader bookshop, bushwalking and travelling.

Peter can be contacted at peter@communitypraxis.org

www.ingramcontent.com/pod-product-compliance
Lightning Source LLC
Chambersburg PA
CBHW062057270326
41931CB00013B/3120